# Butterflies

### Talking with Children About Death...and Life Eternal

## Rev. P. William VanderWyden

TABOR®
PUBLISHING

Allen, Texas 75002

Send all inquiries to:
Tabor Publishing
One DLM Park
Allen, Texas 75002

Printed in the United States of America

ISBN 1-55924-873-4

2 3 4 5 6    99 98 97 96 95

To the memory of my father,

**Peter W. VanderWyden,**

who showed me the two basic characteristics of God's personality—strength and love.

And to all those whose lives have been changed forever by loss—
of a child,
of a spouse,
of a parent,
of a friend,
and who try valiantly to explain *why* to children ... and themselves.

# BUTTERFLIES

# II. TALKING WITH CHILDREN ABOUT DEATH

# III. FINDING SUPPORT

# CONCLUSION

# Introduction—Why This Book Was Written

Tommy* was a beautiful little boy. He was intelligent, with fine, delicate features and a quiet sensitivity. His love for his little brother Bobby was evident, and he was always eager to be helpful.

Tommy suddenly died at the age of six in an accident in his own yard. His death devastated his parents and relatives and stunned our small community. In my first year as the pastor of a congregation, I faced the difficult challenge of providing comfort to the grieving relatives, reassurances of faith to members of the congregation, and explanations for those who doubted the sense of life in the face of such a shocking tragedy.

*Pseudonyms are used throughout the book to respect the privacy of the families.

## A Test of Faith

When a young child dies, our assumptions about the purpose and length of life are challenged by the realization that death can come at any time to *anyone*. Though they have not had a full chance to experience life, death can unexpectedly, unjustly come to our children.

The inexplicable death of Tommy tested my own faith as well. I had officiated at many funerals for older individuals whose deaths were more understandable or predictable. But when a child dies, the unjustness of the event imperils a person's hope that life makes any sense. That is why this book is written: to help adults, whose belief system may be inadequate, to cope with a child's death and to be able to explain death itself to children.

It is a curious irony of this time in history that many parents talk about "the facts of life" with their youngsters, but avoid "the facts of death." Death has replaced sex as a taboo topic of conversation. For many parents, the most difficult question posed by a child is not "Where did I come from?" but "Where do I go when I die?"

Our technological society encourages people to deal with death by using the same procedures it prescribes for everything else—cosmetics and speed. The body is presented in the sterile setting of a funeral home, a brief period of grieving is observed, and then life is expected to go on as before.

Obviously, this process overlooks basic human emotional needs in the face of death. And if adults have an insufficient process for dealing with death, it's no wonder they cannot provide adequate responses to their children's questions.

The leading character in Joseph Heller's *Something Happened* (New York: Alfred A. Knopf, 1974) probably speaks for many adults when he confesses that death is an unresolved confusion that causes great emotional pain:

> *I just don't want to talk to people whose husband, or father, wife or mother or child may be dying, even though the dying person might be someone I feel deeply attached to. . . . Since I don't know what to say when someone dies, I'm afraid that anything I do say will be wrong.*

When the reality of death comes without warning into their lives, most people search for meaningful explanations that will help them to cope and recover. A sound philosophy of life, one that includes dealing with death, is essential to go on with life.

## Insights—To See Eternal Life

Human beings, by their ability to imagine, have a natural gift for conceiving seemingly impossible ideas. This "seeing" with our mind's eyes—with-*in* ourselves—enables us to develop *in-sights* about things we have not seen with our outer-sight! This special ability to imagine what we have not yet experienced gives us the potential to have insight into eternal life, even when it is impossible to know exactly what eternal life will be like. Believing in a better life to come affects our behavior, causing us to live more hopeful, happier, healthier lives.

God often gives people a glimpse of eternal life. The title of this book, *Butterflies,* resulted from a glimpse I had of this other life.

Like many youngsters, my son Billy is entranced by caterpillars. Caterpillars move slowly enough to be caught easily, and you can let them crawl on your hand without fear of being bitten or stung!

Billy found a large caterpillar on our hydrangea bush one day when we were getting ready to begin a family vacation. He came running to show me the slowly crawling creature and said he wanted to keep it. But I reminded him that we were leaving in just a few minutes on our trip and said that we should put the caterpillar back where it was found.

With the enthusiasm and persuasive powers of youth, he convinced me that he would take care of it. In the midst of my hurry and preoccupation with packing the car, I acquiesced. We put the caterpillar in the garage under one of the children's little blue plastic sandbox toys and included a supply of hydrangea leaves.

When we got back from the trip, both Billy and I had forgotten about the caterpillar. When we finally remembered it, several days later, it looked dead. Billy was very upset, so I said we could leave it there and hope that it wasn't really dead.

A few days later Billy decided to check on his caterpillar. We heard him yelling in the garage, and we all came running. Crawling up his leg was a beautiful butterfly, flapping its wings slowly to dry them out. Billy was thrilled by this apparent resurrection.

When Easter came that year, my task was to preach about the possibility of resurrection. I used Billy's "too good to be true" story as an illustration. After Easter worship, many adults shared similar experiences of glimpses of resurrection. The insights I developed through these many experiences have proven invaluable and very helpful to those who have sought to understand the "facts of death" and life eternal.

Those insights were especially helpful when our congregation once again faced the death of a child. This time the child, Cindy, was a toddler, only eighteen months old. Her death was not sudden. From the time she was six months old, her family and our church family lived with the ups and downs of her struggle with cancer.

Cindy valiantly endured major surgery, chemotherapy, and related illnesses. For one year, she made temporary recoveries after each treatment and demonstrated a real will to live, but the tumors eventually claimed her life.

As she experienced each treatment, I came to ache with the suffering of this child as if she were my own. In my profession, I am given a rare access into people's personal lives. I had the occasion to see and be inspired by how Cindy's parents explained their child's illness, and where she went after death, to the girl's four-year-old brother, Johnny.

When I was consulted for guidance as to what to say to her brother or to her young cousins, I did my best on the basis of my own experience, but I found that there were few practical resources available to guide people in talking to children about death.

It was during the last week of Cindy's life that this book began to take form in my mind. Cindy's mother graciously shared with me her experiences and her talks with her son during his sister's illness. These, along with interviews with others who have had similar tragedies occur in their own families, give this effort genuineness.

This book is not intended to be a theological treatise, providing pat answers to real-life problems. Therefore, I have focused on providing relevant and practical ideas based on the firsthand experiences of people who have faced the challenge of death and who have explained it to the children whom they love. It is my humble hope that these experiences will help others, because they testify to hard-won victories of a love that lives beyond the grave and overcomes grief with growth.

## A Resource for Basic Answers

I have found that the insights and suggestions made in this book have received acceptance by people from Jewish and Catholic backgrounds, by those not raised in any particular faith, and by those from a wide spectrum of Protestant backgrounds. The faith of religious people is not blind trust in something for which there is no explanation, but solid understanding that has been molded by real experiences of both life and death.

As a result of my own life experiences with death and resurrection, it became obvious to me that the best title for this book must be *Butterflies*. Just as a caterpillar emerges from the seeming death of the cocoon into a better, more beautiful form, so it is for those whose love overcomes death. No longer earthbound, the butterfly is able to sail upward and look down on its former existence from a totally new perspective.

P. William VanderWyden
Amherst, Ohio
October 15, 1990

# 1. Being Prepared to Talk About Death

*I saw a new heaven and a new earth.*

REVELATION 21:1

Death is no stranger to children. They are exposed to it in everyday conversations, while watching TV shows, or through the death of a relative, a friend, a neighbor, or a pet. It is simply impossible to protect children from something as unpredictable and as universal as death.

# 1  Be Prepared—When to Use This Book

Most people would probably prefer to avoid using a book like this with their children until circumstances force them to open it for suggestions.

For eleven years, Debbie had been a healthy, happy, loving youngster. She was popular with her classmates and her teachers, who all recognized her intelligence and wisdom. One day, Debbie was admitted to the hospital for minor surgery. In doing tests prior to the surgery, the doctors discovered she had leukemia. Within three months, Debbie had died.

Because of the severity of her illness, Debbie was confined to her hospital bed during the last three months of her life. Consequently, she had few visitors. But her mother practically lived twenty-four hours a day during those three months with her daughter in the hospital room. Needless to say, Debbie and her mother had time to talk.

Fortunately, Debbie's mother had an unusually strong system of belief and was able to talk openly and honestly with her daughter about all sorts of topics, including death and the afterlife. Because of her strong beliefs, Debbie's mother was well prepared (better than most parents) to deal with her daughter's questions about life and death. Since death can come unexpectedly into people's lives, it is wise to be like

Debbie's mother—prepared and unafraid to speak about death.

When should this book be used with a child? Begin whenever the child is able to understand its message. It is best *not* to wait for tragedy to strike your family or your community.

## Life's Limitations

It is easier to explain to a child about death when you are in a calm and rational frame of mind. An openness to discuss death in the family encourages children to accept life's limitations as a normal part of existence. The avoidance of death in family conversations only breeds confusion and fear in the child's mind.

It is basically unfair to children to wait for the loss of a loved one before the family begins discussing death at home. When a person, especially a child, is filled with emotions of sorrow, anger, loss, abandonment, and fear, theories and logic may fall on deaf ears. It's hard to listen to rational explanations of death when you are in an irrational state of mind.

When a new baby is expected in the family, children are given time to talk about it and get ready for the addition. In the same way, children must be given time to realize that death does occur.

It is easier, of course, to discuss happy events than it is to discuss sad ones. But unfortunate events do take place, and sadness is a normal emotion—especially in the face of death. By including death in everyday conversations and showing that sadness is an acceptable emotion in the face of death, parents teach their children how to deal with all facets of their emotional life.

## An Everyday Part of Life

In many ways, death is a healthy part of the cycle of life. Everything that dies on earth contributes the chemical remnants of its being to substances from which other living things then develop. When leaves fall to the ground to decay, they help form new soil that nourishes plants and flowers. In that way, the cycle of life continues.

Death is experienced in many ways, daily. These are the losses or "small deaths" Judith Viorst talks about in her bestselling book *Necessary Losses* (New York: Simon and Schuster, 1986). These mini-deaths occur at the end of a vacation or a holiday celebration, when moving to a new town, when old toys are thrown away, during a graduation, and so forth. All of these events signal the end of a relationship. Usually, they are accepted, remembered, and assimilated into a person's life.

Death is an everyday part of life. From all my experience in counseling those who are grieving, it is apparent to me that the families who are open to the fact that earthly life ends in death, and who see death as part of the whole mystery of life on this earth, always deal better with death when confronted by it.

However, many times when I officiate at the funeral of an elderly person, I encounter relatives and friends who are totally devastated by this "unexpected" event. In these cases, death was never seen as a part of life and therefore comes as a shock.

I have also seen whole families who are confronted with the death of a young child face up to their grief, work through it, and find the strength to go on with life. They have lived as a family who knows that death is a regular part of life. They do not avoid noticing death around them.

Often, they have had pets and experienced through them the natural cycle of life and death. Their children have learned that death is a natural part of life. Life itself teaches people how death—even an untimely and unjust death—can be survived and even overcome.

## Observing and Learning from Life

By carefully observing events that occur all around them, people can begin to reflect on life in a way that makes sense of death. This is how people grow in wisdom—by learning from life itself. One of the saddest things to see is a person who has grown older but not wiser and who has not learned from living.

Practicing faith by *not* avoiding life's challenges enables a Christian to develop the habit of learning from whatever life offers. The symbol of Christian faith—the cross—is a reminder of an utterly painful and cruel way of dying. Yet, for those who live that faith, it is a symbol of the triumph of a way of life over death itself!

This kind of faith is not one that requires a person to deny reality! Instead, it teaches a person how to observe life, and to notice the deeper realities that may be missed when life is lived only superficially, in a constant denial of death and the injustices life sometimes visits upon us all.

Families who practice this kind of faith learn to accept and affirm death as a transition to new life. When they are faced with death, they feel the pain of loss and grief, and experience suffering and a sense of finality, but they also realize that life is a gift and that they will survive. People of faith who feel the sting of death know the truth of the old adage, "It's better to have loved and lost than never to have loved at all."

A family that recognizes and affirms in its daily life that every life is a precious gift to be savored also learns to go on with life when that gift is unexpectedly taken away by the events of human existence. Those who carelessly roll through life without nurturing the bonds of love and understanding are the ones who are most shocked when someone passes away. They are the ones who feel guilty for not having spent more time with their loved one, or for not saying, "I love you" enough times.

Dealing with death means nurturing life day in and day out. Taking the time to be attentive to children and to answer their questions *when* they ask them are two of the best ways to strengthen a family's bond of love. Only families that face the hard questions of life together are strengthened by them. When parents, or other caregivers, attempt to shelter children from death, they set the children up for difficult adjustments later in life—adjustments which some never make.

The best time to use this book, then, is in the normal progression of life, when children encounter life and death both in nature and in the context of life itself. Parents and all those who work with children can assimilate this book's insights into their own personal understanding of life and death, and be prepared to answer questions.

# 2 General Guidelines

Sally Norton's grandmother had died. Sally's mother told her she could go with the family to say good-bye to her grandmother at the funeral home.

Sally, aged 10, asked, "What will my grandmother look like in the funeral home?"

Her mother explained that she would look as if she were sleeping. Sally went on to say, "I think I might cry."

Her mother answered, "I will, too. Crying just means that you cared very much for her. But you know, she's all right now. She had a very happy life. She was happy to have grandchildren like you who loved her very much. I'm glad she isn't suffering anymore, but we will miss her. We'll be saying good-bye to her at the funeral home today, but she will be with us always. We won't be able to see her, but her spirit will live on in our memories of her and in how much she loved us."

When children ask questions about death, parents often find themselves groping for answers. This is also true of subjects other than death!

This chapter presents some general guidelines for discussing death that are applicable to most situations. Remembering these guidelines when an unexpected question comes up will help parents or other adults to provide answers children will understand.

## Don't Avoid the Subject

When a death occurs in the family or neighborhood, many adults instinctively react by avoiding any discussion of it. They are afraid that such a discussion would further upset the children or other members of the family. Actually, this is not a healthy practice, because it encourages family members to repress their feelings.

There is really no way that you can hide the fact of death from a child when it occurs. Children have a natural curiosity and need to assimilate what has happened into their other experiences of life. A parent can help children make sense of death by openly discussing the event with them. By clarifying their questions and helping them verbalize their feelings and experiences, adults help children accept the reality of death.

Margaret Adams Greenly, a social worker specializing in working with children whose parent or sibling has cancer, states, "If they [children] don't get told the answer, then they dream up a fantasy instead."

Unfortunately, the fantasy is often more emotionally harmful than the reality.

## Be Available

Questions from children about death seldom come according to a regular schedule, or even when parents are most able to answer them. Children usually ask questions when they cannot figure out the answers for themselves. Then they are anxious for a solution. Teachers who work with children on a regular basis recognize the importance of "teachable moments"—those times when children are at a point where they are eager to understand a subject and are most receptive to learning.

One of the most difficult problems is finding time when parents can be available to respond to the concerns of their children. In many families today, both parents work. And, increasingly, there are single parents who are wholly responsible both for raising the child and making a living to support the family.

Whatever your family situation may be, it is essential that you find quality time when your children have your full attention. When a death has occurred that touches your family, you especially need to be available to your children to help them work through the grieving process.

This may be difficult following a prolonged illness in the family when your nerves are frayed. You may need to find adult support (see Section III FINDING SUPPORT) to see you through a trying time. By meeting your own emotional and spiritual needs, you will be more able to meet the needs of your child.

## Give Honest Answers

Children are usually very quick to recognize insincerity. When they sense someone is being insincere, they push and test the limits to find the truth. It is unwise to make up answers you think the children *should* hear when you yourself do not believe them. You may think you can convince your child, but, eventually, he or she will see through any attempt to sugarcoat the truth.

Children are also quick to judge whether an action conforms or doesn't conform to spoken words. They notice when their experience differs from what an adult tells them. Adults should be sure of their own understanding of death before trying to provide answers to their children's questions. You can only give to other people what you have in the first place.

## Practice What You Teach

Actions speak louder than words—especially to children. So when you share your beliefs about life eternal with children, your actions must support your words. You must act with hope and confidence, and live in a way that tells others that you believe that life goes on after death. The children whom you love will be in desperate need of your strength, support, and attention following a death. You will be in a grieving process yourself. In the midst of bereavement, you must show that life goes on and that your children and the other members of your family need your love and support as much as you need theirs. In a way, you heal yourself when you work to heal others.

The best way to get children to trust what you are telling them is by honestly acting on your beliefs! You do not have to stoically turn off your own emotions. All you need to do is express your feelings honestly and in the context of what you believe. If you believe that life continues in the midst of death, your actions will naturally reveal this attitude.

## Don't Be Afraid to Cry

Many people in this culture, especially men, have been trained to control their emotions and, in particular, never to cry. Being strong is often equated with anger, and tears with weakness. It's no wonder that young boys try to emulate Dad at a funeral by repressing their tears instead of letting them out.

Being open to your tears allows your body to release feelings of guilt, anger, frustration, and anguish. In this way, your body becomes cleansed of pent-up emotions. In *Henry VI*, Part III, Shakespeare says, "To weep is to make less the depth of grief."

Being able to show your feelings or tears to your child is a form of courage. You give your child nonverbal permission to cry. The cleansing power of tears can then get the body's natural healing processes to begin working. You also affirm for your child that life on earth is not always happy or perfect, but that strong people can find ways to deal with crises and challenges.

## Involve the Children

Children are naturally vital and full of energy. It is difficult for them to believe that someone they loved has died. And so they often want to see if the person is really dead or not.

Opinions differ about when a child should be included in funeral rites or services. A funeral is an important rite of passage in a family. It confirms the fact that the loved one will no longer be part of the everyday environment of the family.

Excluding a child from participating in the funeral without good reason could cause her or him to doubt that a death has really occurred. If a child is old enough to have some understanding of what the funeral is and expresses a desire to attend, he or she should be permitted to do so. Margaret Adams Greenly suggests:

> Involve the children to the extent that they are comfortable, including the wake, funeral, and burial. But don't force them to go. If they don't want to or can't, let them do something else if they are old enough, like helping with the flowers or the food so that a child could always look back and feel a part of things.
> Lorain (Ohio) Journal, April 22, 1985

The more emotionally mature the child is, the more she or he will be able to participate in the funeral and be able to comprehend what is happening. However, a child should never be forced or shamed into attending if she or he does not want to do so.

There are some families who prefer cremation to burial, or who believe that the casket should be closed during the memorial service. I cannot argue with whatever religious concept—or sometimes necessity—motivates these choices, but, from my own experience, I believe that not being allowed to view the body can create problems for children and adults. For example, when I was unable to attend the funeral of a beloved aunt, I had an eerie feeling that she was still alive. It was not until I traveled to her home and felt the absence of her physical being that I was able to let go of the feeling.

The funeral process of viewing the body and visitation by relatives and friends can provide positive psychological benefits. It can help grieving relatives and friends to accept the death of their loved one and find healing. Viewing the body need not be regarded as an outdated or tortuous ordeal. Rather, it provides a time to say good-bye to the loved one, and to express how much he or she was loved.

When someone is loved deeply, no matter how long that person's death may have been anticipated, people often say they wish they could have hugged that person more, or said more often "I love you," and expressed how irreplaceable he or she was. A eulogy highlighting the unique exemplary characteristics of the deceased person can help relieve some of these feelings.

Visitation allows individual expressions of feelings and provides a time for those grieving to feel support from friends and relatives. A child may cry at a funeral, but the parent can hold the child in a comforting manner, allowing the child to know that someone is still there for her or him.

Following the funeral service, children should be permitted to be present and participate in any family gathering. Every family works through grief in a different way. At some gatherings, family members may show intense grief, with crying and even wailing. Other families may gather together and recall joyful memories of the deceased.

A child's presence at such gatherings confirms his or her membership in the family and solidifies a sense of belonging. Anything that brings the family together following a death helps to reduce painful feelings of rejection and isolation. For life to go on, death must be accepted. Funeral services and rites help family members do this.

# 3 Working Through the Healing Process

When a child falls down and scrapes a knee, a natural progression of healing usually follows. There are certain actions a caring parent or caregiver can take to help the healing process—cleansing the wound to prevent infections, and so on. Neglecting to do these things can prolong the process.

In a similar way, when a loss or death has occurred, a child (as well as an adult) needs to enter into a process of healing. There are recognizable phases, or stages, in this process. Health care professionals have written about these stages and have assigned various titles to them. A pioneer in the field is Dr. Elisabeth Kubler-Ross, who has written extensively about the process of dying and death. Others have benefited from her experience and knowledge and have also described the healing process, often adding different insights.

From my own experience, I too have noted that the stages leading to healing do follow a certain progression, but the order in which they are experienced sometimes varies; and there are times when a person moves back and forth among the stages.

I have found that the ability to recognize a phase, or stage, as one experiences it is enormously helpful. I have observed six stages of healing in my own life and in the lives of those to whom I have ministered. Recognizing these stages helps us to know that our feelings in the midst of grief are all natural and quite normal. Problems arise only when a person becomes fixated in one of the stages, unable to move toward full recovery.

## Stage One—Shock

The initial emotional and physical reaction to a death is often shock for a member of the family and close circle of friends and neighbors. No matter how expected the death might have been, the utter finality of it often causes general feelings of numbness and separation, as if the grieving person were merely observing events going on all around him or her. Some people feel guilty if they can't cry, and worry about why they can't. Actually, they are using their normal coping mechanism to help them function adequately.

The feeling of shock may be experienced just prior to the death of a loved one. There may be a recognition that the end is near and the person in shock calmly goes about making necessary arrangements.

Or it may happen immediately following a death, when many decisions must be made. The experience of shock actually gives a person the energy to get things done—to arrange the funeral service, to contact relatives and friends, to empty closets or rooms.

Usually, the shock ends after a few days or a couple of weeks. Sometimes, something as simple as having to explain why the deceased child cannot come out to play, or why the dead parent cannot answer the phone, jolts a person from the state of shock into a realization that a loved one has died. Then tears may flow. And sometimes, the grieving person tries to strike a bargain with God.

## Stage Two—Making a Deal

Often, as a loved one is dying or after she or he has died, adults and children try to negotiate with God. Their prayer goes something like this: "I'll be a better person if only you won't let him die," or "I'll never fight with my little sister again if only you let her live," or "Take my life instead."

People who are bargaining like this feel a mixture of desperation and hope. They are trying to make a deal to change what is happening. When carried to an extreme, this behavior blocks a person's ability to deal with, and finally overcome, the loss.

Children experiencing this step need additional love and support, with reassurances they are loved and needed in the family. It is important to realize that children need to feel some sense of control in a situation that seems out of control.

A parent may have to help the child realize that he or she does not have the power to make someone well or bring someone back to life. Some children, especially those who come from a strong Christian background, may think that God will bring the dead person back to life. These children may be secretly praying to God and making their own deals. "God, I promise I will be good if you bring my sister back to life."

Parents and caregivers need to be realistic with children, expressing their belief that the loved one is now alive in heaven and that he or she is happy.

It is not very helpful to tell the child that God wanted the loved one to die. The child may then picture God as wicked or One to be feared. Instead, the parent can tell the child that the loved one who has died will always be with him or her, but now is being taken care of by a loving God. If the child comes to believe that the loved one is safe and happy, there will be less need for making a deal. Instead, the child will be free to concentrate on living, instead of denying what has happened.

## Stage Three—Denial

Sometimes, a person is unable to accept the fact that the loved one is no longer around. Particularly when a death has occurred suddenly, disbelief is a form of denial.

The refusal to acknowledge the death by keeping the loved one's room exactly the same, or feeling compelled to make daily visits to the grave, are extreme forms of denial behavior. Obviously, it is important to move beyond this stage. Allowing a child to view the body and participate in the memorial service or funeral rites is a good strategy to use to work through denial.

A parent may have a difficult time accepting the death of a child, a spouse, or an elderly parent. If a parent is in the state of denial, unable to express normal emotions, unable to cry or grieve, other children may feel confused. Children depend on their parents to help them form an opinion of the world and to make sense of the unknown.

To help a child make sense of death, the parent must first be helped to move beyond her or his own denial. Support groups, help from friends and other family members, and counseling from a priest, minister, rabbi, or trained therapist, are all helpful.

If you are reading this book to help you explain a death to your child, you are probably not in the state of denial. If you are a friend or relative of someone who has experienced a significant loss, you can help your friend break through denial by being honest and open about the situation as you see it.

Once a parent is able to deal with personal denial, he or she will be better able to analyze the child's reactions. If the child is in the state of denial, he or she may be going on with life as if nothing had happened. Such behavior may seem callous to adults, but it actually signals the enormous grief the child is trying to ward off by making believe that the loved one is still alive.

Regressive behavior is a less obvious form of denial for a child. A five-year-old child, for example, may revert to baby talk. Or a junior high school youngster might begin to act up in class or do poorly in school work in which he or she once excelled.

All are indications that the child or youngster has not yet accepted the death and is in need of a great deal of love and support to be able to come to grips with it. Regressive behavior may also indicate that the child is about to slip into depression.

## Stage Four—Depression

Depression is one of the best-known stages in the grieving/healing process. In this phase of the healing process, a person feels lost, discouraged, and confused. The depressed person may feel that life is not worth living. Making decisions becomes difficult. Often the depressed person withdraws and avoids contact with other people. Frequently, depressed people say they feel trapped and unable to climb out of what seems like a deep black hole. The void created by the loss seems unfillable; time seems to drag on.

Those who feel guilty because they think they have neglected their loved one, or because they believe they are being punished by God, often endure prolonged periods of depression. Many people feel guilty because there is nothing more they can do for the person they have lost.

When children experience depression, they often think that they have been abandoned because of their bad behavior. Very young children often speak impulsively. If a child has told a loved one, "I wish you were dead," the child might later think the wish actually caused the death.

Chronic depression following the death of a loved one is often anger turned inward—a response to feelings of guilt. In reality, the depressed person is blaming himself or herself for the loss. In such a depression, the normal vital energy of life is turned inward and bottled up; there is no energy, only a feeling of being deadlocked, hopeless. The depressed person may stop eating or perhaps eat too much. Sleeping patterns become disturbed, and personal appearance may deteriorate.

If the depressed person is a parent of small children, he or she especially needs to get help in order to be available to the children, who might naturally fear the loss of another person. But even small children can experience feelings of depression. Behavioral changes in children after the death of a family member or close friend are fairly common.

Whether the depressed person is a child or an adult, it is not helpful to tell him or her to stop feeling so glum and get on with life. Professional counseling may be needed. At the very least, a depressed person needs to be surrounded by gentle, caring people who can provide an ear to listen and a shoulder to cry on.

Since the depression may be a result of unrealistic thoughts or expectations of one's self, a caring person will try to reassure the grieving person that there was nothing he or she could have done that would have changed the outcome.

Helpful work in psychology over the past few years suggests that changes in the way a person thinks ultimately lead to changes in feelings and action. Depressed people habitually tell themselves negative things. If you can help a depressed person stop thinking that he or she could have done more to help the dead person or that he or she caused the death, those negative feelings will lessen, and the person will become more actively involved with life.

Another way of helping the person break the chains of depression is to encourage the depressed person to openly express his or her anger.

## Stage Five—Anger

A grieving person might become angry at someone, including the person who died, or even at God. Anger is a very basic emotion, and obviously a very energizing emotion. Denial of anger and the consequent loss of energy only deepens the listless feelings accompanying depression.

Those who feel anger is a sin or it is somehow wrong to get angry at God or other people become locked in depresosion. Realizing that anger is a basic human emotion and part of the healing process will help to bring the angry feelings out into the open. Our loving Creator knows this and will not hold these feelings against a person who expresses the anger in nondestructive ways.

A child or adult who is struggling with the loss of a loved one may show anger too. The child might refuse to go to school, or get angry at a sibling or a neighborhood friend. It is even possible that the child may blame a parent for the death of another parent or sibling. "If Mommy had been around when Bobby was near the pool, he would not have fallen in and drowned."

An adult might even blame the hospital or doctor for not having done enough to save the deceased, when actually the doctors did all that was humanly possible to make the sick person comfortable and to restore him or her to health.

The hardest anger for a grieving person to express is an anger that is directed toward the person who died. A child might wonder how a parent, brother, or sister could have left her or him all alone. This anger is especially felt in the case of suicide. "Why did she have to kill herself? Didn't she know I loved her?" Once more, anger and guilt are intimately tied together.

A spouse might be angry with a deceased partner for leaving him or her with all of the work or with bills to pay, children to raise all alone, and so on. A parent might even get angry at a child who has died. "If only Roy had listened to me and taken better care of himself...."

A caring person who wants to help a child or adult through the healing process will not be overly concerned about this anger. Instead, he or she will listen to the feelings expressed and accept them in a nonjudgmental fashion.

Once the anger is out in the open and is recognized for what it is, a bereaving person is closer to accepting the death and to returning to everyday activities. From this perspective, anger is a nondestructive, cleansing, energizing behavior and a hopeful signal that the person is nearing the final stage of healing—acceptance.

## Stage Six—Acceptance

If a person has been able to work through each of the stages of healing discussed above, he or she eventually begins to accept what has happened and is able to go on with life. When a loss or death has been accepted, a person is once again able to give of himself or herself, and affirm that hope and happiness are possible in this life. The focus begins to shift away from the loss. The person stops trying to make deals with God, is no longer deadlocked in depression, has stopped blaming himself, herself, or others, and begins to focus on life and the living. The void can now be filled by caring for others.

Children exhibit acceptance by resuming regular activities with a new gusto. A parent might show it by realizing that the children, or a spouse, need attention. The recovering person is able to remember with fondness the one who died, knowing that his or her life has been enriched by the person who has died.

## A Word of Caution

It is easy to put these six stages of healing into neat boxes and assume that all one has to do is go through the stages in logical progression. That's not how it works. More often, a grieving person jumps back and forth between stages, day to day and even hour to hour.

It does no good to repress any one stage when one is trying to recover from a loss. Repressed feelings have a way of resurfacing later in life at inappropriate times. They are more difficult to deal with at those times because the source of the feelings is camouflaged.

Healing is possible, but it is wise to remember that a wound can be reopened. A person may go through all six stages of healing and enthusiastically reenter life. Several years later something may happen to reopen the wound. A person who has successfully negotiated the six stages of the healing process, however, will need less time to recover from an old wound.

Being aware of the healing process and the stages of that process, coupled with a knowledge of the guidelines for explaining death to a child (as previously explored), can be a tremendous advantage to parents and caregivers. Being able to negotiate these stages and help a child do the same enables both to develop a mature attitude about life—one which leads them to affirm that death is part of life and that life continues after the death of a loved one.

# II. Talking with Children About Death

Tears may flow in the night,
but joy comes in the morning.

Psalm 30:5

# 4 Different Ages, Different Approaches

When talking to children about death, try to approach them at their own level of understanding. No matter how well-intentioned a parent is when explaining death to a child, a youngster needs to hear the message in words he or she can understand and assimilate. Otherwise, the child will feel frustrated, confused, and sometimes angry.

My experience and study indicate that different approaches are needed for *infants and toddlers* (under the age of three), *preschoolers* (between the ages of three and five), *primary school children* (between the ages of six and nine), *preteens* (between the ages of ten and twelve) and *teens.* Each age group has its own psychological and spiritual needs and its own unique way of making sense of the world.

It is helpful to be aware of these differences and to be able to apply knowledge of a child's development to explanations about life and death. The ideas offered here can be used more wisely if you are aware of how children at different ages of development can relate to death.

## Infants and Toddlers

Even a child in his or her mother's womb can experience the sting of death. Research has indicated that a fetus does monitor and respond to the emotional atmosphere surrounding the mother.

After birth, growing infants are influenced by the important caregivers in the family. From infancy, toddlers know what it feels like to be separated from someone they love. For them, death often feels like abandonment or removal from a source of security. Loving adults can appreciate a child's need to be hugged and to be given special attention in the event of a death in the family.

Toddlers, of course, cannot yet fathom the meaning of death and probably will ask when the absent person will come back. To answer them, it is best for caring adults to calmly and slowly tell toddlers that the loved one has gone but still loves them.

Toddlers might not be able to understand everything that is said, but if they hear an answer that is given in a confident manner, followed with a sincere expression of affection—an embrace, a kiss, or a sympathetic smile—they will feel secure. The expression of love and affection communicates on a non-verbal level that the child will survive the death of a loved one and will not be abandoned.

## Preschoolers

There are several ways of helping preschoolers cope with the reality of death. If a parent, or other close relative, dies during these preschool years, the model conversations in Section III of this book will provide guidelines for the adult who is trying to help the child cope.

When a death occurs in the family, it is usually appropriate to include four- or five-year-olds in the funeral process, if they express a desire to participate. Viewing the body will help them accept that their loved one has actually died. If the adults around them act in a confident and loving manner, funeral customs and rites will not scare the child.

Children are naturally centered on themselves at this age. When a parent dies, a young child might wonder who will take care of him or her now that the parent is gone. The child may also become increasingly concerned about the surviving parent. Such children need to be reassured in simple language that the surviving parent's health is fine and that she or he will take care of them.

Because language skills are still developing, a child in this age range might communicate her or his feelings through bodily symptoms and complaints, instead of through words. If someone in the family was ill for a long period of time and then died, a young child might complain that she or he is not feeling well. The child might say, "I'm not hungry," or "My tummy aches." The child might also mimic the physical distress of the deceased person. It is best in these situations for the parent or other caring adult to be as patient and reassuring as possible.

## Primary School Children

Primary school children are just beginning to develop a moral consciousness. At this stage of development, they begin to reason. When someone in the family is ill or has died, children of this age often wonder if they were responsible and then feel guilty. They may spend a lot of time thinking about what they might have done to cause the illness or death. It is important for a caring adult to listen to children surface any concerns and to reassure the child. The simple facts of the illness that led to the death can be explained without going into distressing details.

When a death has occurred, children in this age group should be told immediately, in familiar surroundings, by loving parents or caring adults whom the children know well. Again, physical expressions of affection will help the young child more than any words.

At the time of death, young children will feel the loss deeply and yet may not be fully able to comprehend death as a natural process of life. They can learn to accept the death by being involved in the funeral rites and in the visits to the cemetery.

During these visits, talk calmly and patiently about what has happened and point out that the cemetery is a special place to feel closer to the loved one. This will help heal the wounds and will facilitate recovery.

Do not be afraid to show your own emotions, but be careful to let your child know that you are confident that things will get better in the future and that together the family will survive. If the dead person is cremated, you may wish to place the ashes in a particular place or develop a special prayer that enables the child to feel close to the loved one.

Older youngsters in this age range are usually more outspoken and often have the ability to perceive reality more clearly. Of course, children who can read will have encountered death in various children's stories; or will have seen death portrayed on television. It is important for parents to be available to answer their questions as they emerge.

## Junior High/Middle School Youth

Most young people in this age group will seem to understand the explanations offered to them; but at the same time, they will be filled with the same fears, anxieties, panic, and guilt experienced by younger children when someone close dies.

These young people often identify with other people, including their parents. When someone in the family has died, a preadolescent might begin to assume the mannerisms of the deceased person. If the deceased person was a brother or sister, there might be some family pressures—usually unconscious—to act like him or her or even to take the place of the deceased.

When you realize this is happening, it is important to encourage the young person to be himself or herself and not to assume the additional burdens of trying to be someone else. It is wise to remember that these young people are at a very important developmental stage and need kind, patient love and attention to help them acquire a mature attitude about morality, life, and death.

## High School Youth

In this culture, it is surprising how many youngsters reach adolescence without having had a significant experience relating to death. So, unless the young person has had to deal with the death of a parent, grandparent, sibling, or friend, parents can often unwittingly keep their children shielded from the facts of death. Often this is a defense mechanism used by an adult who has personally not assimilated death into his or her own view of life.

Adolescence is a very difficult time of adjustment to life. It is a time of great emotional mood swings and, often, hidden insecurities. A young person who appears very strong still needs the regular loving encouragement and support of the family group. Thus, our young people need to feel they are not enduring their adjustments alone. Even though they have been encouraged to develop a strong sense of independence, young people need our support and openness to discuss opinions and life experiences.

The keyword in dealing with young people in this age group is *availability.* At this difficult transition time in life, availability of parents and those who can empathize, at the time of the day-to-day crises of adolescents, is essential! Adolescents need to recognize that no matter how alone they may feel, God is always there, not judging them, but available to confide in, and to give help and strength and love, and to forgive ... always.

The problem of adolescent suicides must be mentioned. Nationally, suicide among these youngsters is increasing at an alarming rate. It is important for parents and other caregivers to be aware of this serious problem and to demonstrate compassionate understanding at this crucial time of development. Be alert to any changes in your own son's or daughter's behavior. If he or she becomes moody, changes his or her patterns of sleeping or eating, begins to talk about death a great deal, and starts giving away valuable possessions, seek help from a school counselor, a therapist, or a priest, minister, or rabbi—someone who is competent in dealing with this problem.

At a time of death, help your son or dauther express his or her feelings, whether they are anger, grief, sadness, or bewilderment. Probably the most important gift you can give your teenager at this time in his or her life is the priceless gift of a listening ear and an understanding heart.

# 5   Responding to Questions About Death

One day, my son Billy asked me, "But, Daddy, nobody in our family will die, will they, Daddy?" This probing question came up unexpectedly as Billy and I were riding in our car on the way home from church. Earlier in the morning, Billy had seen his friend Johnny in Sunday school, and it must have gotten him to thinking.

He had begun the conversation by saying, "You remember when Johnny's little baby sister Cindy died, Daddy?" And when I answered affirmatively, he went right to the question about death and how it could affect our family.

At the time of Cindy's death, about three months before this conversation, my wife and I had spoken with Billy (then four years old) about our understanding of death. We had assured him that Cindy was all right now and that she was in God's keeping and not suffering anymore. Now, for some reason, three months later, Billy was concerned about whether people in his family would die.

As anyone who has contact with children knows, this is a typical example of how a child's attention functions. Children are constantly absorbing and assimilating all sorts of information about life. Adults who love and care about them must be prepared with answers to help them understand during those teachable moments, when children ask questions and seem most interested.

## Use Your Own Words

This section provides answers to common questions children and young people ask about death. The explanations are straightforward and to the point. They are written on an adult level, because it is vitally important that adults interpret the concepts in their own terms. Then they can honestly, comfortably, genuinely, and sincerely explain the facts of death and eternal life in their own words—in a way children will trust.

Those who contributed stories and experiences to this book have faced the loss of people they loved and have successfully met the challenge to accept death as a fact of life. They believe and trust in the promise of eternal life, rather than doubting that life makes any sense. The ideas, concepts, and guidelines suggested in this section reflect that positive belief.

## Eight Common Questions

As parents will tell you, the question most frequently asked by children is "Why?" Children have a basic, innate need to know the "why" of things.

One of the questions most threatening to faith is "Why did this happen to me?" The question takes many forms for adults. "Why did I lose my job?" "Why doesn't anyone like me?" "Why isn't my life working out the way I want it to?" "Why should I believe in God when the world is in such a mess?" "Why are people so cruel at times?" "Why is my child—or spouse—dying?" "Why did he or she die and leave me all alone?"

These "why" questions express the ultimate concern about the purposefulness of life in general and of individual lives in particular. To answer such questions for children, adults must come to grips with their own explanations. Children of today no longer will accept "This is just the way the world is, and you have to have faith that God wanted it that way." Pat answers are *out*.

I have found the following explanations to be helpful to adults and children who are trying to understand the meaning of life and death. I offer these, written on an adult level, so that parents and other interested adults might weigh them against their own experiences and use them as practical approaches to helping children better understand the mystery of death and eternal life.

Each explanation responds to one of eight questions commonly asked by children about death. As you read and consider these questions and explanations, keep in mind that you can impart only what you truly believe yourself. Feel free to accept the explanations, modify them to suit your needs, or reject them.

The important point is to develop your own understanding of life, death, and life eternal. Then you can share your thoughts with your child in your own words and in words your child can understand.

### Why do people die?

I have found four concepts that suggest answers to the "why" of death.

**Death is part of life.** There is a piece of German wisdom, *Ein teil des lebens ist die sterbe nur,* which means "Death is only a part of life." This proverb was used during the memorial services for Ted Leimbach, who died at the age of twenty-one in a head-on auto collision.

Those who knew this young man felt robbed by his untimely death. His mother, Pat, a nationally syndicated columnist, wrote the tribute, which effectively captures Ted's vital spirit. In talking about Ted's death, his mother wrote:

> *It doesn't seem enough to say of our Ted that he was born and that he died. It helps us in our grief to call up his twenty-one years and recognize them as rich,*

*full, and exciting. We can only be grateful then that*
*we had the joy and the privilege of sharing those too-*
*brief years, of loving and encouraging Ted in the pur-*
*suits that did him honor....*
"In Celebration of the Life of Ted Leimbach"

In his short lifetime, Ted Leimbach had shown a real zest for life. He filled his short life with many activities and achievements. Looking at his whole life from this perspective, it can be seen that his death was only one part of his life.

Ted's full life can help us realize that the one day of his death should not outweigh all the other days and positive events of a person's life. In the midst of grief, people often let death have a disproportionate emphasis on the way they look at a life.

At such a devastating moment, we must work hard to not let the events of the death overshadow the experience of the person's life. It is helpful to remember that the death occurs on only one day of the person's life, and that there are many preceding days of sharing, joy, and courage.

To have the opportunity to live and experience the joy of giving and receiving love is a gift in itself. So, as Pat Leimbach illustrates in talking about her beloved son Ted's life, she remembers all the high, inspiring moments, and does not let the one day of his death carry a disproportionately heavy emphasis in relation to the rest of his life.

In other words, when evaluating a person's life, in the face of death, you must look at the whole picture and see that death is only one part of life. It is not the length of a person's life that determines its significance, but what happens during that lifetime.

***Death reminds us that life is precious.*** The suddenness of Ted Leimbach's death left a great void in the lives of those who loved him. This great sense of loss, which occurs whenever someone who is loved dies, provides a second clue to the meaning of death—life is precious.

Death reminds people that life is a precious commodity! Since no one lives forever, life is best lived when each moment is savored. Ted was the type of person who was able to do this. In *Harvest of Bittersweet*, (New York: Harper & Row, 1987) his mother described his enjoyment of life:

> *A two-year-old, standing in his crib grasping for a sunbeam.... A little boy with an elfin face, serious and humorless, slightly pigeon-toed, pushing a tractor in a sand pile, discovering he had a motor, "bbrrr...." A father's constant companion, on his lap or on the fender or beside him in the cab.... A cocky little second baseman in a felt cap.... Hail fellow, well met, Joe College of Agriculture coming home from ag con class... World traveler going off to Austria... A gung-ho mini-bike rider, and on every Sunday a trophy for a centerpiece... triumphant as the number two American at the International Six Days in Germany.*

Ted knew how to live and enjoy life. In a truly spiritual sense, when anyone stops growing or takes life for granted, he or she begins to die.

It might be said that wasting time by not caring for someone or something is a form of slow suicide. Perhaps the best use a person can make of time is to care for other people.

Death shocks us into realizing that loved ones will not always be around. When death claims the life of a loved one, it often prompts the survivors to draw closer together. In this way, perhaps death serves a positive purpose, reminding people to not take life for granted.

The most important lesson parents can teach their children is that life has value. By making family time a high priority, by offering frequent expressions of affection like hugs and kisses, by saying "I love you," and by listening to their questions, feelings, and ideas, parents demonstrate to their children that life is indeed precious.

***Love overcomes death.*** When someone experiences a death and feels the loss deeply, it is not very comforting for them to be told that life is precious. They realize that fact from firsthand experience. The event of death has occurred and there is no more time left to care for and love the person who has died. Any satisfying response to the death of a loved one must touch the heart as well as the mind.

Love is the only satisfying answer that overcomes the finality of the fact of death. Death is the ultimate challenge to the power of love to overcome life's limitations. Perhaps the "why" of death is so that love can show its power.

Paul Tillich, the internationally renowned theologian, in an essay titled "Love Is Stronger Than Death" in *The New Being* (New York: Charles Schribner, 1955) explained:

> *Who can bear to look at this picture [of death]? Only he who can look at another picture behind and beyond it—the picture of LOVE. For love is stronger than death. Every death means parting, separation, isolation, opposition, and not participation. Our souls become poor and disintegrate insofar as we want to be alone [in our grief], insofar as we bemoan our misfortunes, nurse our despair, and enjoy our bitterness, and yet turn coldly away from the physical and spiritual needs of others. . . .*
>
> *Love overcomes separation, creates participation . . . love is the infinite which is given to the finite.*

I have discovered that God's love comes in the midst of death when you turn outward from your grief. Although the loved one who has died cannot be replaced, someone is there to love.

When grown-ups see the pain that children feel at the time of a death, they cannot help but want to reach out to care for them and give them the love that will enable them to go on with life.

Normal human limitations are extended whenever a person can sacrifice his or her own needs and desires to care for someone else. Life then becomes worth living and a glimpse of eternity is experienced.

By giving that special feeling of being valued and appreciated, love enables people to feel that their unique lives have a lasting significance. Meaning can be found in the most unfair of life's events.

*Death is the end of suffering.* Accepting death and integrating death into life is part of the maturation process. When death hits home and a child becomes involved in the processes of mourning and recovery, the question of the "why" of death truly emerges.

When children see loved ones suffering before their eyes, they realize that death is not always as swift or antiseptic as it is often portrayed on television or in the movies. When the suffering is especially prolonged or painful, it is quite common to hear family members express their hope that the loved one will soon have the release of death, so he or she will no longer have to suffer.

These hopes are often accompanied with some twinges of guilt. But such hopes can also be an expression of a deeper understanding of what life is all about. Death is the end of suffering, and when one has endured pain, death is not necessarily an unwelcome event.

This can be true in the case of a child's death, as well. Children who are about to die often are aware of this fact. Sister Margaret Sheffield, a member of the Sinsinawa Dominican Congregation of the Most Holy Rosary and a staff chaplain of a hospital in Alaska, reported the following words of a dying child to her doctor:

> *That's the very last time you are going to prick me.*
> *From now on I will not let you put another needle*
> *in me. I'm so tired of all this. It won't ever do a bit*
> *of good. All I want now is to go to heaven. I'm just*
> *waiting. Why does God make me wait so long?*
> *I'm all ready to go.*
> Living Light, June 1987, page 341

I often remind families whose children have experienced great suffering before dying not to let the suffering blind them to the lasting inspiring things of life—the courage, joys and laughter, the happy memories of times spent together. Those who believe in a better life after death will view the end of a temporal struggle as a time of grace.

Young children who ask, "Why do people die?" need to be reassured that God did not cause a parent's or sibling's death. They need to hear tht God is taking care of their deceased parent or sibling, whom they still love deeply.

### What is God like?

It is difficult to describe God. The use of such theological words as *Almighty*, Creator, and *Provider* clearly are not adequate when trying to explain God to children. To be accurate, it cannot even be said that God lives, because living as experienced on earth is defined by the conditions of temporal existence, which has limits, beginnings, and endings. God's existence has no limits!

The problem is further compounded when children hear such cliches, especially at times of death, as "God wanted your friend to be in heaven." Such expressions give children a confusing image of God. On the one hand, God is supposed to be all-loving, but at the same time, God seems insensitive and self-serving.

The Hebrew people were the first to believe in a God who overcomes death. From the beginning, that belief set the Jewish people apart from the rest of humanity. Surrounded by tribes and people who ascribed god-like qualities to the sun, the rain, the moon, the wind, fire, or other elements of creation, the Hebrews insistently clung to their belief in one God, who created everything and who cared for them.

Describing the nature of this one God, however, is very difficult. When there is only one God, even if we mention all the different parts of creation, we cannot fully encompass the Creator of all. When Moses encountered the Divine Presence and inquired how to address God, the only answer he was given was, "I am who am."

I interpret this to mean God's "being" is revealed by the actions God displays. The characteristics of God, who is revealed through actions, can be described with "action" words, just like the attributes of any human being's personality. Therefore, God can best be described as loving, forgiving, merciful, providing, just, peacemaking, hope-sustaining, death-overcoming.

Perhaps the best and the most tangible illustration of God—albeit insufficient—is in the actions of loving human beings, because men and women were created in the image and likeness of God, able to understand right and wrong, and free to love or not.

Younger children often need a more visual explanation of God. For example, I am reminded of the story of a mother who saw her child making a very unusual picture, and asked what the child was drawing. The child responded, "God! I'm drawing God."

The mother said in surprise, "But no one knows what God looks like!"

"They will when I'm done!" the child responded.

For children, the very best way to describe God is in terms of a loving parent. Like a good parent, God helps people, provides for them, and gives them freedom to make choices. Of course, this metaphor has limitations, especially when the child does not have a solid experience of a loving parent. For most children, however, it helps to anchor God in images the child has experienced.

For Christians, the most accurate and complete illustration of what God is like is found in the life of Jesus of Nazareth. Jesus lived a life that was Good News to those who needed strengthening in their belief in the power of a God who loved them, hence the four stories of his life are called *gospels*, which literally translates as "good news."

Jesus, as described in the Gospels, reveals God by forgiving others, being merciful, healing those who were sick, and bringing hope to people in despair by overcoming the conditions of the world, even death!

I often meet people who have doubts that Jesus is the son of God. We generally assume that children act like their parents, so I ask them, "How do you think the Son of a God who is loving and self-sacrificing would act?" In my estimation,

Jesus lived the kind of life that we would expect of a son of a loving God.

Jesus lived a life of loving everyone, no matter what their heritage or background. At the same time Jesus was strong in that love. He demonstrated what was good for people and what was unhealthy. Those are two basic characteristics of the God we see described in the Bible—strength and love: *strength* to protect and guide us, and *love* to forgive us, love to care enough to sacrifice for us to overcome the limitations of the world.

So, when children ask "What is God like?" the best answers are, "God is like a loving person" (Jesus is our best model for this), or "God is like a loving parent."

### What is a soul?

How would you explain exactly who you are to someone else? As part of my work as a pastor, I have had to write many eulogies. In the process, I have discovered that trying to summarize the special and unique qualities of any person is an impossible task. A person's life and personality cannot be summed up in words.

Little children, with their basic energetic drive, have difficulty accepting the fact that life has limitations. Therefore, when a death occurs, it is not easy for them to accept. If a parent or other adult attempts to comfort them by saying that the soul lives on, most children will wonder and ask "What is a soul?"

In simple terms, the soul can be described as that which gives us life and makes us a unique person—the unique energy of each human being.

The leaves of trees provide a good metaphor to help us explain the nature of our souls. In autumn, we revel in the beauty of the leaves turning a multitude of beautiful colors. But actually, those beautiful colors have been hidden in the leaves during the summer!

The lush green is created by chlorophyll, which, with plenty of sunlight and carbon dioxide, enables the tree to produce starch and sugar and to grow. The green of the chlorophyll in the leaves, abundant in the summer, masks their true colors.

Then with the shorter and cooler days in the fall, with less sunlight, the process of photosynthesis diminishes, and less chlorophyll is present in the leaves—and their hidden beauty is revealed.

Similarly, our souls are not immediately visible, but our true, unique essence shows through, no matter what physical characteristics we have. The soul makes it possible for people who may appear to be rather plain to be fun to be around, or to have "that something" that is beyond appearances. Conversely, some people can be physically very beautiful, but their self-centered personalities make them unattractive.

The metaphor of the leaves can be taken even one step further. When the leaves are virtually dead, and have fallen from the living tree, their beautiful "souls" are revealed. So it is that we believe our beautiful souls live on in a better form.

Another way to explain the nature of a soul to a child would be to talk about the difference between a house and a home. We watched our present home being built from the ground up. Each day we saw the different parts of the building being put together, the fixtures added, and so on.

Then one day the contractor said, "You can move in, probably in a couple of days." Never having experienced this process before, I innocently felt that there were some special ingredients that would be added those last few days that would change it from a building to a house.

But all that happened was that the carpeting was installed and everything was sort of cleaned up, and we were told we could move in. I felt that there should be some switch that would be flipped so it would become a "working" house, in the way you assemble a motor and it's immediately ready to run.

Having seen each of the parts of the house installed separately, I hadn't realized that the sum was much more than the parts. The furnace was running before the house was finished. The electricity and lights were turned on as the workmen installed appliances. So there was no switch to turn on, yet all the parts together made a house!

But it was still just a house, not a home. It wasn't until we moved in all our furniture and personal possessions that it began to feel like our home. Even then, for me, it took a while before the house felt like home.

Eventually, the rooms began to become coupled with feelings about experiences we had had in those rooms, and the whole thought of the house was associated with warm feelings of family activities. In a way, the house developed a personality as unique energy was derived from the activities that it made possible, that gave it the aura of a home.

The feelings that make a house become a home could, I think, be likened to the relationship between a body and a soul. In explaining the soul to children, you could use the example of the process of a house becoming a home.

A converse example might work best if you are trying to explain death and a soul. If the children have experienced moving from one house to another, you could remind them of how empty the house felt when all your furniture and possessions had been removed. That hollow feeling could be likened to the hollowness we feel when looking at a loved one's body in a funeral home. Often, the deceased look as if they are just sleeping, but their cold, quiet immobility reminds us that the energetic, vitalizing soul has left the body.

You might also reassure children that after death the person lives in a new way—like the butterfly! The concept of a soul is also helpful to use in explaining that our loved ones are, in a way, always with us after death. My father, Peter William VanderWyden, passed on to life eternal in 1970. Our first child, Billy, was not born until 1979. So he and our other three children never had the privilege of knowing their paternal grandfather.

But in many ways, his soul is alive with them. They know what he looked like from photographs. But making even more of an impression on them has been what I have told them about him—his strong love, his courage, his confidence, how he enjoyed his work, how he loved to ride horses, how he took our family on vacations. They have heard about his love from their grandmother, from his two surviving sisters, and other relatives.

Perhaps more directly, they have a sense of what he was like by some of the ways I act, as I've striven to emulate his most admirable traits. And I have told them how much he would love and enjoy being with them.

Sometimes, I notice that they talk about him with the energy and affection we use when we talk about someone we like and who we know loves us. In a very real sense, my father's soul is an important part of my young children's lives and their hopes and dreams for the future, providing a great heritage for their lives. And I am sure that his soul will be around in their children's lives as they tell them about him.

Even those who doubt the resurrection of the body do admit the fact that people who have lived loving lives and who have made contributions to the world live on, at least in the memories of others who loved them. Their inspiration and example last beyond their death.

Conversely, everyone knows at least one person who stopped giving of himself or herself and who simply withdrew from life. These people seem to be dead before their heart stops beating or their brain stops functioning.

A person's soul reflects his or her ability to love, and this ability puts a person in touch with eternity.

*Love puts people in touch with eternity.* When you give generously of your life's energies, or sacrifice yourself for the welfare of others, you put yourself in touch with eternity.

Love is the one thing that comes back as soon as it is given away. All other possessions are susceptible to the conditions of death—deterioration, breaking down, wearing out, or being destroyed.

Whenever one loves another person selflessly, a chain of good feelings begins to link people throughout the world, and this chain promotes belief in the basic goodness of life.

Only a person who has experienced love firsthand knows what it is. Once the power of love has been experienced, a person realizes his or her own self-worth and importance in the world. When unleashed, this power permeates all of existence and helps the soul to realize its true potential—to connect a person to eternity.

*Human beings are created to live forever.* Because human beings are created in God's image and likeness—capable of loving and being loved—human beings are meant to live forever.

The soul is the essence and core of a person's being. The yardstick of eternity does not measure a life by the number of years a person lives on earth, but by the contributions a person has made to the world and by how much a person loves and is loved. Contributions to the world do not necessarily refer to great acts of public service. A person contributes to the well-being of humanity simply by living and trying the best one can to get along with other people.

A belief in the soul can be a wonderful blessing to a parent whose child has died. An infant evokes love or a desire to love in other people. This is one of the many ways babies and children show love. By inspiring their caregivers to be more loving people, children make lasting contributions to their family and to the world.

To summarize, a soul is the vital energy of a being that gives life to its body and unique qualities to its personality. When the soul is missing, the body of the being is dead. But people of faith believe that if a soul has been loved and is able to return love according to its own means, it can be resurrected to eternal life.

### How long is eternity?

One topic that always brings a host of questions from adolescents in my Confirmation classes is eternity. They have heard the word, but they do not understand it. Indeed, for most people, the concept of eternity seems beyond understanding. In this temporal world, everything that happens has a beginning and an end, so to imagine an endless existence seems difficult—if not impossible!

I suspect that part of the reason people don't understand eternity is that the only place they regularly hear about it is at church services. There, the clergy usually speak of it in awesome, hushed tones of reverence, presenting it as a mystery that must be accepted at face value.

Some people are afraid to think about eternity or question its reality in any way. They just believe that everyone will spend an eternity in either eternal bliss or eternal damnation. Because this kind of belief may breed fear and anxiety, many people either avoid thinking about eternity altogether or even reject the idea outright. But actually, the thought of eternity can be comforting and can instill hope in people who have lost a loved one through death.

Ordinarily, human beings think in terms of beginnings and endings. A person is born at a certain place and time, lives for a period of time, and then dies. A young child begins school, later graduates, and that ending is a beginning of another stage of life. Projects are begun and then finished. When they are not finished, there is a feeling of incompleteness.

Both scientists and scholars of religion hold that there was a beginning to earthly existence. The Book of Genesis starts with "In the beginning. . . . " Modern scientists offer the "Big Bang" theory to explain the beginning of the world.

Philosophers and those interested in religion move beyond the question of earthly existence when they raise the question, "What happened before the beginning of time?" This question leads to another one—"What happens after the end of time?" Both of these questions reflect the more personal questions—"Where was I before I was born?" and "What will happen to me when I die?" Both children and adults have wondered about these two questions.

Some people look to the theory of reincarnation to answer these questions. Still, the question remains, "What happens after the last reincarnation?" For Christians, eternal life is a more satisfying answer than reincarnation. Imagine that you could construct a spacecraft that exceeds the speed of light, and you journey to the *very end*—to the farthest edge of the whole universe. You are faced with the question, "What is on the other side of the edge?"

Then you find yourself entering into another universe and you reach its edge. Again, you wonder, "What is beyond all of this?"

Clearly, the human mind finds it difficult to conceive of dimensions beyond beginnings and endings. And yet, that is what eternity is all about. Think, for a moment, of the circle, which obviously has no beginning and no end. To make the concept three dimensional, imagine a hollow sphere or an imaginary ball whose surface is made of *time!* By definition, a living being exists through time—from second to second, minute to minute—living, breathing, moving, and changing. Without the concept of time, it is impossible to speak of a living being.

To make the time-sphere more real and personal, imagine each person's life forming a dot or a line somewhere in the circle. Where is God and eternity in this time-sphere? You can find God right in the center.

God is present throughout time and history. Although people live in different eras and cultures, lifelines cross and people connect. In fact, by drawing lines on a sphere, a person can have a visual image of the complexities of human interactions. Some religious traditions speak about a *communion of saints* to explain how people from different times, different generations, and different cultures interact with one another.

When someone who has been exposed to the power of love dies, that person joins God within the center of the sphere and thus overcomes time. There is an end to earthly existence, but not an end to existence itself.

People of faith are comforted by the thought that existence does not end with death and that they will be able to see their loved ones again. It is personally comforting for me to know that I am already in some way reunited with my Father.

At the same time when the bereaved miss and are yearning for the loved one, they are actually already united with him or her. It is only from the perspective of being on the outside edge of the time-sphere, living an earthly existence, that waiting is experienced.

With God, the waiting is over. In fact, it never began in the first place. Beginnings and endings merge into one another. This reality is expressed in the Book of Revelation when Jesus says, "I am the Alpha and the Omega, the first and the last, the beginning and the end" (Revelation 22:13). In Christ, the living and the dead are connected to one another in a spiritual way.

### Is there a heaven and a hell?

A survey, which found that 80 percent of Americans believe that when they die they are going to heaven. Probably if people were asked to describe what they mean by heaven, there would be a variety of responses. It is even possible that some people would have had a hard time putting into words their concept or image of heaven.

The results of the survey did not surprise me. The belief that God is loving and forgiving is much more prevalent today than it was in earlier times, when God's judgment was emphasized. "Hellfire and brimstone" sermons have given way to a preaching style that focuses on a loving God.

What I did find surprising was the fact that so many people believed in heaven. The 80 percent of people who reportedly participated in the poll far exceeds the percentage of people in our country who identify themselves with an organized religion.

It seems to me that the poll reveals an attitude that assumes that a person will go to heaven if she or he has lived a moderately good life—not especially virtuous—and avoided evil. In my opinion, this nonjudgmental attitude is just as superficial and harmful as the "hellfire and brimstone" attitude of former days.

In my opinion, a more meaningful approach is to define heaven and hell in terms of life experience. Simply put, hell is the state of living without the presence of love. It is possible for a person to make his or her very own hell on earth—by becoming selfish to the point that everything done is self-serving, with no consideration for anyone else's needs. A self-centered life-style builds walls of coldness and isolation that cut people off from one another and create individuals who are unable either to give or receive love.

Heaven, on the other hand, is the state of living and participating in love. Love puts people in touch with eternity. The familiar phrase "love lasts forever" reflects this notion.

At those special moments in life when a person feels miraculously and unconditionally loved, time seems to stand still. When someone is able to love another person in an unselfish manner, the good feelings that follow provide that person with a small taste of heaven.

Heaven can be seen only with the heart. In the popular children's story *The Little Prince,* a wolf tells the little prince that the kind of friendship that truly bonds people together is something that cannot be seen with the eyes, but only with the heart.

The same can be said about heaven. Heaven is *not* attained by living merely respectable lives and following all of the rules.

Heaven comes to people who recognize their humanness and their need for love. It is impossible to "earn" heaven.

It is given as a gift of love, which must be accepted. Only the person who goes beyond trying to save himself or herself and who accepts being loved and forgiven by God can understand and look forward to the promise of heaven.

Heaven is wherever love can be experienced with the heart. Conversely, hell is not so much a place but when the heart has grown so cold that it can't see or feel love anymore. Simply put, when a person dies, heaven is the state of being in the presence of love. In the First Letter of John, it is written:

> Whoever does not love does not know God, for God
> is love.... This is what love is: it is not that we have
> loved God, but that God has loved us.
> 1 John 4:8, 10, slightly adapted

In heaven, a person experiences a sense of wholeness, and of having eternal significance because God's love is so overwhelming.

### Why does God allow people to kill?

According to the theory of evolution, the law of nature is the survival of the fittest. Predatory animals kill other animals to get the food they need to survive. Plant-eating animals compete and fight for food, and those who are best adapted to their environment prevail. Although it is usually upsetting for a child to see one animal kill another animal, as seen on a television nature program, the behavior can be explained in terms children understand.

Explaining why people kill other people, however, is a more difficult task. Human beings have the ability to know what is right and wrong, and know what it feels like to be hurt. Human survival is not usually dependent on killing other people for survival. So, when a person's life is abruptly cut short by a killing, intentional or not, children, friends, and relatives are left wondering if there is a caring God in charge of the world.

How can a loving God allow good people to die—especially at the hands of another? This question becomes especially painful when a child dies at the hands of a child abuser, or when innocent people are killed during wartime. To people who believe that God is all-powerful, it may appear that God has withdrawn from involvement in human affairs and has permitted all sorts of atrocities to occur.

Humankind's inhumanity to humanity is evident throughout history. In the ancient world, warring tribes slaughtered whole villages and nations, including women and children—often to gain possession of land.

For many centuries, in biblical times, the Jewish people were at the mercy of the Roman officials who taxed them unmercifully and often persecuted them as well. After the death and resurrection of Jesus Christ, the Roman Empire often tortured the Christians in the Colosseum, leaving parents and children to be devoured by wild beasts.

In modern times, recent wars have claimed the lives of countless men, women, and children. The world came close to witnessing the near genocide of the Jewish population in Eastern Europe during World War II.

Innocent people, including children, were killed indiscriminately during the Vietnam War, and the human carnage continues today in places like Ireland, the Mideast, Africa, and Central America. Some movies, such as *The Killing Fields*, depict the senseless and atrocious slaughters that make sensitive people wonder where God is hiding.

Killings are reported daily in the newspapers. Children of the screen generation are confronted with violence and mayhem on TV and in the movie theaters. Because of modern technology, thousands of children saw a rocket explode in midair one February day in 1986, and soon discovered that the lives of seven astronauts, including a schoolteacher, were snuffed out because of a mechanical defect that should have been located and repaired before blastoff.

While children are taught about God's love at church and in the home, they are confronted with the world's suffering and pain on a daily basis. In these times, especially, children and adults must wonder how a loving God could allow such things to happen in the world.

The most basic answer is that God loves us so much that we have total freedom to make our own decisions. Each person is created by God to be a free moral agent in the world. We can use our freedom to love or abuse our freedom and hate. The only other option would be for us to be like animals and not know right and wrong, or to have limited choices that would relegate us to the level of puppets.

As a gift freely offered, God's love can be refused. But God knows that real love can occur only in an atmosphere of freedom, where it is given willingly, not out of duty or compulsion. Therefore, in the midst of such freedom, people can choose to love or to hate, to help or to hurt, or even to kill.

In dying willingly on the cross, Jesus showed the great love of a Son willing to take on undeserved suffering to show us the cruelty and futility of killing.

George Burns, portraying God in the movie *Oh, God!* says, "I've given you everything you need. You can either hurt and kill each other or help and love each other." That is really the message of the biblical story of Adam and Eve. The story is not really about the creation of man and woman "eating an apple," but about the choices confronting human beings.

Of all the animals created by God, human beings alone have the ability to choose between right and wrong. The story of Adam and Eve symbolizes the first time sin was introduced into the world by a wrong choice on the part of human beings. Some people have trouble understanding this story, because they think it must be interpreted literally, in physical terms. But, as in many of the stories in the Bible, its truth is seen in what it symbolizes.

It was not a sin to eat an "apple." But by disobeying the guidance of God, who, like a loving parent had provided everything that was needed, human beings made an ultimate choice. In a way, going after what they were told was not good for them, Adam and Eve rejected the bountiful love that was provided; and their sin was the rejection of the love, the injuring of their relationship with God.

My definition of sin is "behaviors that are detrimental to loving relationships or to human beings individually." By choosing to disobey God's commandment, human beings took upon themselves the burden of the responsibility for making choices, and the agony, and limitations, and suffering that came with living away from God's abundant providing.

God loving us totally allows us to have this freedom to choose, because God has the wisdom to know that true love must be voluntarily given, not forced. The story of Adam and Eve is an enlightening metaphor for the limited, free world we live in outside of the Garden.

This story in the Bible is followed by another that symbolizes the basic truth of the foolishness of killing. In the story of Cain and Abel, brother is pitted against brother, and envy leads to murder.

These stories were probably told by parents to respond to their offspring when they asked the question, "Why does God allow people to kill one another?" These stories then were passed on from generation to generation, and improved upon along the way, until they became ritualized and accepted as basic stories about why the world is the way it is.

### Why does God allow suffering?

The Greek playwright Aeschylus wrote, "He who learns must suffer, and ever in our sleep, pain that cannot forget falls drop by drop upon the heart, and in our despair against our will comes wisdom, by the awful grace of God."

Throughout history, a religious question that has been raised over and over again is: "Why does a supposedly caring God let people suffer?" This is the most basic question that can be raised about the relationship between love and life.

It is an especially poignant question when a loved one is chronically in agony. "How much can God care if someone who has basically tried to live a good life is in such pain?" If adults ask this type of question, they certainly will be at a loss when trying to provide a satisfactory answer to their children.

One approach taken by many adults is to resort to a stoic view of life. They say suffering must be endured by one's strength or willpower. Bad things simply happen in life! The celebration of good times must be tempered by the thought that one must always be prepared for suffering. This approach is obviously potentially harmful to both adults and children, since it robs life of any joy.

There is a modern proverb: "Don't pray for an easy life, pray to be a strong person." This presents a more positive alternative to stoicism. Like the stoic approach, it emphasizes a person's strength of character, but it does not repress feelings or deny the experiences of joy and exuberance life has to offer in addition to suffering.

I do not think that God wills suffering to happen, but I believe meaning can arise from suffering, when a person has the strength to meet its challenges. By overcoming suffering, we develop character and that most important characteristic of Christians—confidence!

Although I do not believe that God causes or even wills suffering to happen, I do believe God's love is present to those who suffer and to those who must watch a loved one suffer and even die. The love and grace of God can help a person survive painful times and become a stronger person through the ordeal.

The Apostle Paul describes how a person who has opened himself or herself to God's love might respond to any of life's tragedies:

> We are often troubled, but not crushed; sometimes in doubt, but never in despair; there are many enemies, but we are never without a friend; and though badly hurt at times, we are not destroyed.
> 2 Corinthians 4:8-9

In the Christian tradition, Jesus reveals a God who stands by people—especially people who are suffering. Compassion is one of the many attributes used to describe God in both the Hebrew and Christian Scriptures. The word comes from the Latin *pati* and *com,* which together signify "to suffer with."

No, God does not cause the suffering of humankind. Instead, a compassionate God suffers with those who endure pain.

The fact that God's son, Jesus, died on the cross shows us that God has experienced human suffering firsthand. Whatever we suffer, we can remember that God is there, too; and because God is with us, we can overcome our suffering.

Friends and relatives who help us through the grieving process with their presence and their prayers, and their hugs and tears, are showing God's love through their actions. When we feel empty, having lost a loved one, they can help us heal by surrounding us with love, so that we can go on, regain our strength, and love again.

In a Christian community, following Jesus' example, people share one another's sorrows and suffering, and thereby show that Christ is still alive and has overcome the ultimate suffering of death and grieving.

Even when we feel alone or abandoned by others in our suffering, if we fremember that Christ is our constant companion, we can find comfort and peace in our spirits and can hope to persevere and to overcome our suffering.

***But why me, God?*** When a person faces a crisis, tragedy, or some extreme form of suffering, the normal human response is often, "Why me?" In the midst of suffering and grieving, there really is no adequate or satisfactory answer, because in our pain, thinking does not reach our emotional need.

In his popular book *When Bad Things Happen to Good People* (New York: Schocken, 1981), Rabbi Harold Kushner grapples with the question of suffering and pain. But I think an even more interesting question is, "Why do *good* things happen to *bad* people?"

When a person is suffering or watching a loved one endure immense pain, it is only natural to look around to see other people prospering with good health, fortune, and countless blessings. Sometimes it seems that these people are not as good, or as loving, or as hard working as those who suffer.

Often, people who are mired deeply in despair feel totally alone and perhaps even abandoned—by God and by others whose lives seem more joyful at the moment. Frequently, a sick person or someone suffering a loss or tragedy sees his or her pain as being unique. Consequently, the suffering individual often withdraws from friends and neighbors and experiences feelings of isolation and alienation.

The only real cure for the loneliness of suffering is to get out of yourself and become involved with others. Sometimes the best people to become involved with are those who have shared a similar tragedy in life.

By having compassion for others who are also hurting, you can transform your self-concern into an inner strength that supports others in a moment of pain. When you can summon up the courage to share another's pain, you often find that your own begins to diminish. "Your pain is the breaking of the shell that encloses your understanding," says Kahlil Gibran in *The Prophet.*

In turn, others can be a source of comfort and support for you as well. Suffering is a human bond, enabling us to empathize with one another and to realize we need one another's help and companionship.

Why are people able to be loving to others? Usually it is because they have suffered also. A sympathetic person understands what a person in pain is going through, but an empathetic person knows firsthand what it feels like.

I think that is what the crucifixion of Jesus was all about. God became human and entered the world as Jesus, and willingly suffered injustices, persecution, and even death. Jesus knew firsthand what it feels like to be rejected, abandoned by friends, and to be in great physical pain.

Jesus reveals a God, whose care is genuine. In Jesus, God knows what it means to be human and to suffer the tragedies that life often brings upon people, often unexpectedly and undeservedly.

From my own experience, I have found that joy and pleasure are more fully appreciated when suffering and pain have been endured. Actor George Burns, portraying God in the film *Oh, God!*, in explaining suffering and joy says, "I never could figure out how to make anything with only one side."

Somehow, when a person is able to come through a crisis and find release and relief on the other side of it, he or she is more capable of experiencing joy. Mysteriously, the height of joy is in a large measure determined by the depth of despair one has experienced. Kahlil Gibran in *The Prophet* says it this way, "Your joy is your sorrow unmasked. The deeper that sorrow carves into your being, the more joy you can contain."

The love shared by two people who have been married for a long period of time is an excellent illustration for understanding the connection between pain and joy. Having lived through the struggles, trials, conflicts, and tests that come with intimacy, a married couple develops a special and close understanding of each other. Each partner has faith in the other and knows that together they can experience joy and overcome pain.

Suffering is not really something that can be explained away with easy answers. It is something that must be lived through and survived.

A materialistic and idealistic society tends to want to shelter children from all types of suffering. Parents don't want their children to be deprived or to be hurt in any way. When children are overprotected or provided for in abundance, however, they may grow up and find an adult world for which they are ill-prepared.

The fact is that it is not possible to eliminate human suffering totally from life. Suffering is a basic condition of human existence. It is universal—a given. No one has ever gotten through life without knowing some form of suffering. No one ever will.

Suffering, in its essence, is the supreme test of life! When people suffer, faith in God and in life are questioned, and sympathy and love are put to the test.

Religious faith, however, informs those who suffer that the Creator can help them in the midst of their ordeal. God shares in the plight of human beings who suffer. That is the meaning of a God who hears the cry of the afflicted (see Exodus 2:23-24), and a God who, in Jesus Christ, overcame death on the cross (see Luke 24:36-45).

Jesus died to let people know that God willingly takes up the pain and suffering of humanity and shares in it. The Christian way of life is not an easy way. God did not promise to remove our problems, but did promise to be with us and help us deal with them. People of faith realize that the only positive response to suffering is to go on with life and to believe that suffering can be survived and overcome.

Those who believe in a God who suffers along with them or who follow Christ may not be guaranteed pain-free lives, but they know they do not suffer alone.

I have come to realize that suffering can have a positive effect on human beings. This is felt in three ways:

*Suffering makes people realize they need one another!* Because suffering is universal, no one needs to feel alone in his or her pain. Suffering provides a special opportunity to get to know another person intimately. Whenever someone cares for another person and shares the struggles life often brings, he or she comes to recognize one's own weakness and need for human contact.

I know that every major trial I have lived through in my own life has made me more sensitive to how others hurt, too.

Because I have suffered, I can truthfully say, "I know how it feels," and remain confident that the other person will sense the genuineness of my caring. I am a better minister because of my suffering. I realize I need other people and that other people need me.

***Suffering leads to learning.*** When things are going well in life, there is often a tendency to take things and people for granted. But suffering shatters complacency. When tragedy strikes in any form, it forces people to assess what is truly meaningful and precious in life. Confronting death reminds people that life does not last forever.

***Suffering teaches that death is not the final word.*** When suffering comes in the form of death, the pain can be excruciating. And yet, the sting of death can be healed—and through that healing, people learn that death is not the last word. The Christian Scriptures reveal a God who is not content to let death be the final word on the unfairness of life. With the passion, death, and resurrection of Jesus Christ, God provided the one lasting solution to life's greatest tragedy. Life is to be found in the midst of death.

### Why do people say, "Keep the faith"?

"Keep the faith" is an expression that has found popularity among many people. It is a simplistic reassurance often spoken whenever someone is faced with hardship or a challenge. Often, it refers to faith in yourself, the team, life itself, or even fate.

When someone dies, the faith that is needed is quite a different kind of faith. When a loved one dies, more than self-confidence is needed to recover. Often, the death of a loved one makes a person feel as if a part of his or her very own self has also died. "To have faith is to be sure of the things we hope for, to be certain of the things we cannot see" (Hebrews 11:1). The ability to see beyond death and to learn to live with it requires this kind of faith.

In modern culture, influenced by the scientific world view, the word *faith* has become a confused and misunderstood concept. It is important to identify two things faith is not!

First, faith is not a convenient arrangement with God in which eternal life is the reward for a successful life. This kind of misunderstanding finds its roots in the Protestant work ethic that has so influenced American habits. Anyone who puts in a hard day's work is entitled to a decent and fair wage. If you don't work hard, you run the risk of being fired or losing a portion of your salary.

Scripture, however, describes God's love as being given as a gift of grace—neither earned nor deserved. Eternal life is the gift of a loving God who cares for human beings whether or not they are deserving of love. This kind of faith inspires people to live good lives out of a sense of gratitude rather than a fear of not gaining eternal life.

Second, faith in eternal life does not lead us to deny reality and to believe only in something for which there seems to be no logical, scientific explanation. Faith can be strengthened and find roots in our experiences.

I believe in life after death because the major experiences of my life have shown me that love is far more dependable than the tangible things in this world. Machines wear out and break down over the course of time. Material possessions often lose their ability to interest consumers after their initial purchase. Fortune and fame do not last forever.

And yet, the beauty of God's created order prevails. The dead of winter is followed by the return of life in the spring. Miracles often occur in the midst of tragedy. People endure great pain and suffering, recover, and lend their support to others. Healing is possible where love prevails.

These are some of the experiences that suggest to me that the hope of eternal life is a very real promise. Ralph Waldo Emerson said it well when he wrote, "Everything I see of God's creation convinces me to trust in him for what I have not seen."

In other words, to have faith means you realize what is really precious and meaningful in life, and you let that be your reassurance of God's love for you. This kind of faith can take you through very difficult times, helping you see the light at the end of what seems to be a very dark tunnel.

After you realize that faith is not a convenient arrangement with God or an act of willpower, you will be able to see that faith is basically a long-term trust.

Confronted with a death, keeping faith is what you do while you are waiting to be reunited with a loved one in heaven. Faith is really the only positive response to death. It means deciding to live with hope instead of despair. It requires cherishing memories that inspire you to go on with life and to recapture the happiness and joy that the dead person would want you to have.

Those who decide to choose life—instead of isolation and loneliness—after the death of a loved one find healing. When they are finally able to stop dwelling on the pain inflicted by the loss, these people begin to return to the land of the living and find that other people need their love and need to love them in return.

When a death occurs in a family, children inevitably ask questions. A parent or other loving adult answers these questions more through actions than with spoken words. When adults have a long-term trust in the promise of eternal life, which enables them to go on with life, their children learn that life is indeed worth living and that death has little real lasting power over people.

This kind of faith is exemplified in the life of professional baseball player John Candalaria, whose son nearly died in a drowning accident. While his son was still in a coma, Candalaria was able to say, "That's what faith is. You have to believe before you see!"

In the deepest sense, faith means being able to go on living with a hopeful attitude, even in the midst of death. Faith enables those who are grieving to regain a sense of humor and a joy for living. It is able to do this because of the promise of eternal life and the hope that one day people of faith will be reunited with those whom they have lost to death. Faith takes the sting out of death.

# III. Finding Support

*There shall be no more night, and they will not need lamps or sunlight, because the Lord God will be their light. . . .*

Revelation 22:5

The primary focus of this book is on children and on how to help adults explain to children the facts of death and life eternal. But, of course, the feelings and needs of the adults who try to explain—and console—cannot be ignored. It is not always easy to console another person—even a child—when you are grieving yourself. First you must find support for yourself and a way to cope with your own sorrow.

# 6   Coping with Your Own Sorrow

When a child's grandparent dies, a parent not only has to explain this death to the child, but also must face the loss of a parent. If a child's mother or father dies, the surviving parent must help the child accept the loss and, at the same time, learn to live with a great void in his or her own life. When a child dies, there are often other children for whom the parent must provide a sense of love and security.

And, the parent must deal with a multitude of conflicting feelings—sorrow, anger, hurt, confusion, guilt, maybe even relief. No matter how much parents may feel an obligation to put up a strong front for their children, they cannot deny or repress their own feelings if they are to recover.

If parents are not able to handle their own grief, all the explanations in the world—as excellent as they may be—will fail to help children understand the facts of death and life eternal.

There are several strategies parents can use to cope with their own feelings of loss. These strategies fall into three categories: (1) professional counseling or talking with friends, (2) peer group support, and (3) self-help methods. Each of these three strategies will be considered separately.

## Professional Counseling and Talking with Friends

Just as children need to discuss their feelings of loss with their parents or other significant people in their lives, adults also need to discuss their own feelings with people whom they trust. Since death causes people to confront basic questions of life, it is usually a mistake to think a person can deal with those questions alone.

Of course, many people attempt to do just that, perhaps feeling that it is a sign of weakness or emotional immaturity to admit they themselves need help to cope with personal anguish. This is especially true of many men in our culture, and with both men and women in some ethnic groups.

All human beings who have any sense of caring or commitment to people around them experience stress and strong feelings of loss when someone close to them dies. Hiding those feelings will not make them go away. Often, if the feelings are not faced and met squarely, they will surface sometime later when other traumas trigger them; or they will lead to some kind of compulsive or addictive behavior that camouflages the real feelings.

Engaging in open conversations with others about what one is going through can provide a cathartic and healthy way to sort out feelings, enabling them to become a means to growth. In the process, one's understanding of life becomes more profound.

For many people, talking with friends or relatives is an easy and comfortable way to share the painful experience of a death in the family. When people dare to disclose their personal thoughts and struggles, they find other people who have been there, too—people who can provide great comfort and counsel from their own experiences.

Consider using the wisdom and compassion of an understanding parent, aunt or uncle, cousin, or good friend to help see you through a trying time. Most friends and close relatives expect to be informed of your need for support. Sometimes, acquaintances whom you respect and trust may be just the people you need to confide in.

It's best not to assume automatically that people don't want to be bothered with your problems. In reality, most people are flattered and honored to be consulted under such circumstances. Often, people gain new insights into their own struggles with life when they try to help a fellow human being. I have found this to be true in my own life.

If you do not feel that you can confide in your friends or relatives, or if your struggle with pain and loss is more than you feel you can bear, consider seeing a professional therapist or counselor. There are many from whom to choose. Great care, however, should be taken in choosing a counselor. Some counselors even specialize in the grieving process.

How do you go about finding a good therapist? The one place where you do not want to begin your search is in the yellow pages. Someone may have great marketing skills but not be a good counselor.

Often, your family physician or friends and relatives can be of assistance to you in locating the right person for your needs. If your pastor, minister, or rabbi does not have a background in counseling, she or he should know the names of qualified professionals who can help you. Begin by asking people whom you trust for recommendations or referrals. You might want to obtain the names of two or three people.

You will want to be sure that the counselor you choose is properly trained. You might find yourself confused by the many different professional degrees or credentials you will find when looking for a counselor. Professional counselors include psychiatrists with M.D. degrees; psychologists with a doctorate in their field; counseling psychologists who may have at least a master's degree in psychology or education; social workers; marriage and family counselors; and priests, ministers, and rabbis who have pastoral counseling skills.

Whomever you choose, there are some specific things you should look for. As with any other profession, there are competent and incompetent practitioners. Begin by checking the person's training and background. It would be helpful if she or he had specific training or substantial experience in helping grieving people. You will also want to know what fee is charged and what times the counselor has available for appointments.

During the initial consultation, ask how long the counseling might take. The stages of healing are somewhat predictable, but each person moves through them in his or her own way and time. A counselor's services, however, should not be needed for more than a year, unless other problems complicate the situation. I am distrustful of therapists whose time lines for counseling are too open-ended. Often, they seem to create dependency needs in their clients and patients.

If, after you begin counseling with someone, you do not feel you can trust or open up to her or him, seriously consider switching to someone else. Remember, your goal is full recovery and participation in life. You have a right to choose the person who can best help you achieve that goal.

## Peer Group Support

Many community health centers, parishes, congregations, and hospitals offer grief recovery groups. There, people who have experienced the tragedy of loss can gather together and share their sorrows with one another without feeling embarrassed. In the process, people who support and help one another find ways to overcome their grief and get on with living life fully.

There are many ways of finding such support groups. Many metropolitan areas have coping hotlines that you can call and be given the phone numbers or addresses of support groups in your area. Even smaller cities and rural areas have local newspapers that print this information on a regular basis.

Two good places to contact for this information are local hospitals and neighborhood churches or synagogues. They might even sponsor such groups at their own facilities. If you have ties to a faith community or are searching for a spiritual way to overcome your grief, contacting your pastor or rabbi would be a good way to begin.

Your own parish or congregation might not have a grief recovery group itself, but the pastor or rabbi might know of a group that will respect your religious outlook and value system. Or your faith community might have other groups that could help you understand and talk about your grief more fully.

Prayer groups, Scripture-sharing groups, or general discussion groups sponsored by your parish or synagogue may not focus specifically on loss but would be open to helping you deal with your grief.

Actually, a faith community is a good place for healing to occur. It supports an environment where people come together and generally make a commitment to share in one another's joys and struggles.

My own congregation is like a large, warm family whose members regularly support one another at times of loss. In such a large family, there are many people who have gone through the painful experience of loss and who have survived.

They are often the best resources for helping others through similar experiences.

One specific group we started in my church was a parenting group. Freely admitting that parenting is one task at which everyone begins as an amateur, the group members gather monthly to hear a variety of professionals who regularly work with children—pediatricians, school psychologists, psychiatrists, youth workers, teachers, clergy, and the like—talk about different topics.

People from all segments of the community, many not members of our church, have found this to be a very helpful forum. On specific occasions, the group invites someone to speak on illness, death, and grieving.

If your church or synagogue does not have such a group, you could ask your priest, minister, or rabbi to help you begin one. The pastor or rabbi could invite all those who have been bereaved in the last year or so to come to the first session.

There is an international organization consisting of local chapters that could give you some ideas for starting a group of your own. Compassionate Friends was founded in Coventry, England, in 1969 by Reverend Simon Stephens, an Episcopal priest.

Parents who have suffered one of life's greatest tragedies—the death of a child—often come together on a regular basis to express their pain, cry out their anger, weep for their child, and tell their stories. Information about starting one of these groups can be obtained by contacting Compassionate Friends, P.O. Box 3696, Oak Brook, Illinois 60522-3693.

## Religious Groups

Besides comforting people, churches and synagogues also offer rituals to help people express their feelings in a prayerful manner. Good liturgy always helps people perceive and put into perspective their lived experiences.

Jewish people usually hold a funeral on the day after the person dies. The body is washed, dressed, and placed in a plain coffin. The mourners cut a slit in their outer clothes to show their grief.

The coffin goes first to the synagogue and then to the cemetery, where the rabbi and others speak about the dead person. At the end of the service, the relatives fill the grave with earth and the closest male relative prays the Kaddish.

For seven days, the mourners sit *shiva*. Each day, services are held in the home and friends bring food and comfort to the grieving. In this way, the community surrounds the mourners with love, helping them to express their grief within a religious ritual.

Christians generally hold memorial services, wake services, and funerals. During these services, there are readings from Scripture, eulogies, and songs. Protestants often come together in the church for the memorial service, where the whole congregation, church family, shares in the suffering, support, and hope. Catholics normally gather together with family and friends and take part in the celebration of the Mass. Members of the community often prepare food to serve to the mourners after the funeral service.

In my own experience, people often tell me that the very personal eulogies offered during a memorial service—mentioning courageous, humorous, and exemplary times in the loved one's life—are a real source of comfort and hope.

Examples of good wake services can be found in Josephine Massyngbaerde Ford's *Silver Lining: Personalized Scriptural Wake Services* (Mystic, CT: Twenty-Third Publications, 1987). In general, all such religious services offer a group or community experience of shared grief, where people help one another, through ritual, to deal with feelings of loss and sorrow, as well as to give hope to the survivors.

## Self-Help Methods

In addition to friends, professional counselors, and group support, there are many other ways you can help yourself deal with grief. Reading this book is a beginning. Prayer, helping others, reading in general, and participating in rituals are other ways to help you recover and go on with life.

A high-school counselor, writing in *The American Journal of Nursing* (March 1978), stresses that "grief takes many forms. . . . Each person must find his or her way of handling it. . . . You can't always be busy, and you must eventually be alone to face your loss."

*Praying.* One powerful way to help yourself cope with death is by praying. This should be an obvious choice in the face of death, but often, people who have prayed throughout their lives find it difficult to pray following a loss. They get caught up in the anger or depression stages of the healing process.

They might direct their anger at God, whom they feel took away their loved one. Logically, they may realize this is not true, but the feeling nevertheless persists and colors their thoughts and actions. To them, God seems to be the best scapegoat under the circumstances.

Other people who are afraid of anger, especially anger at God, might sink into a depression and blame themselves and feel unworthy of God's love or attention.

Those who never attended church, or who stopped participating in church activities years ago, may feel unworthy to pray. Agnostic doubters might see death as the confirmation of their suspicions that God is either uncaring or nonexistent. These people may see prayer as a futile exercise that makes them feel foolish.

Prayer can help those who grieve, no matter what their circumstances in life. Whether a person feels angry or depressed, unworthy or foolish, prayer is an appropriate response to loss. It is an effort at communication and can be done by using any means of expression.

Prayer does not have to be done quietly while you are kneeling with your eyes closed. It can be done by yelling or crying, with eyes looking up to God or cast down to the earth where your loved one is buried. God can handle your anger. Through prayer, feelings are expressed and healing takes place.

The Book of Psalms is a good place to begin. Anyone who reads the Psalms cannot help but notice that many of them were written by people who were angry with God, as well as by people who cried out to God for help. Because these prayers are found in the Bible, believers can be confident that God accepts a variety of human emotions and the ways in which we express those emotions.

The lament psalms show people how prayer serves as a catalyst to healing. Often, this kind of psalm begins with the speaker crying out in anguish or rage; for example, Psalm 137. This is followed with a plea for God's help, and by the end of the psalm, the speaker voices gratitude for God's never-ending love or expresses confidence that God will indeed act.

Praying the psalms serves several functions. First of all, it is cathartic. The prayer of the psalms is perhaps the one place left where all feelings and thoughts can be laid on the table. It is speech that allows people to discover the power, extent, and intensity of their hurt or pain and gives them a way to express these feelings.

Second, the psalms legitimize one's feelings. Through this kind of prayer, people discover that words, feelings, and thoughts do not destroy, nor does God get angry at their expression. The pray-er does not have to act out anger and rage. The speech itself releases these feelings and leads to a transformation of them.

Finally, in yielding to a hope that God will act, the psalmist is liberated. The feelings are transformed and the one who cried out goes on living.

Perhaps the most important thing prayer accomplishes is liberation. Prayer always changes things, but what it changes the most is not the situation but the person who prays! Over a period of time, perhaps through the process of daily prayer, a person changes in how she or he looks at life.

Prayer gives everyone an opportunity to pause and reflect on life's events from a variety of perspectives. From such meditation, a new way of looking at life and death gradually emerges. The person who prays begins to notice how God and other people care, calling him or her back into life. Prayer ultimately gives the one who prays the courage to reenter life and live it more fully.

*Helping Others.* Another way to help yourself is by helping other people. I often tell people who come to me for advice, "Get out of yourself and into other people."

This does not mean that I expect them to deny their own pain and suffering. I merely suggest that they transcend their own pain and suffering by helping others who, in some way, are also distressed. I suggest this self-help remedy because it enables people to see that they are not alone in their misery.

Others provide good company because they share some of the same hurts.

Reaching out to others in need gives one's own pain a new meaning. It becomes a way of connecting with other people and, at the same time, forces the mourner to do something creative with his or her own pain.

I discovered the rewards of keeping busy and helping others after my father's death. I was my father's only son, born late in his life when my father was in his fifties. For this reason, perhaps, my father had always made me feel very special and loved by him, and I responded in kind. When you are loved unconditionally for who you are, it is easy to return that love.

At the time of my father's death, I was living alone in my own apartment. I wanted to withdraw from life and just lie in bed, pounding the headboard to express my anger and feelings of helplessness, grief, and pain. But I was also a schoolteacher with responsibilities and was doing full-time graduate work, studying in the evenings for a master's degree in sociology. I had to prepare my lessons, go to school each day to teach, study and go to class each evening. It was the busiest schedule I ever set up for myself.

During this time, I felt I should think about my father, analyze our relationship over the years, and remember the good and the bad times we shared together. But I was much too busy to do half of the meditating I wanted to do to honor my father's memory.

I soon realized, however, that my self-imposed schedule of work and study was the wisest thing I could do. All the analysis and the thinking about my father in the world would never change what had happened or bring him back to me. The only action worthy of his memory was to go on with my life, to become the contributing member of society that he had raised me to be.

In much the same way, parents who survive the agony of losing a child must direct their energies to the remaining children, who still need their love and attention, or to others they love.

Parents have a responsibility to their children, as well as to themselves and to each other. Children and other loved ones remind those who grieve that they are still needed, that life must go on. In time, the focus must shift from what has been lost to what (and who) is still left.

A death in the family can be an invitation to grow and meet the challenges life offers you. Besides the other people in your life who need your care and attention, there are probably many responsibilities, challenges, and activities to occupy your time and energies.

One woman whose husband died in his early fifties had to learn how to drive a car for the first time in her life. This activity helped her overcome her grief and redirected her energies back to the task of living.

To help her children go on with life, this woman began to do things, such as ice-skating, she hadn't done in years. In the midst of great pain, this family found comfort in one another and were able to survive the death of a husband and father.

If someone in your family or close circle of friends has died and you feel overwhelmed with grief, try to look at your life in a broad way.

Who is still around who needs *you?* What are your talents, abilities, or resources? Can they be put to use in some way? Are there people in your neighborhood or community who could profit from your skills or abilities in some way? Is there a project you can get involved in? What are your current responsibilities? Are you fulfilling them? Responding honestly to these questions may be just the thing you need to do to push you back into life.

*Reading.* There are many books on the market that talk about the stages of death and dying. These books can prove to be quite helpful to people living with a dying person, or for people who have experienced a death in their family or circle of close friends. Some of the most helpful books have been written by people who lived through the experience and who were courageous enough to share their feelings and insights with other people. One such book is *How to Survive the Loss of a Love* (New York: Bantam, 1983).

Another book *When Parents Die: A Guide for Adults* (New York: Penguin, 1986) written by journalist Edward Meyers gives practical advice on the sadness of watching elderly parents die. The effectiveness of this book lies in the author's methodology. He used a questionnaire that he circulated among friends, relatives, and people throughout the United States. The book is filled with stories from people's own experiences of watching someone they love die.

*Butterflies* itself was written out of a similar need. There weren't many viable practical resources on the market that could help parents explain death to their children. This book was written to meet that specific need, and includes insights and suggestions from people who actually lived through the death of a close relative—usually a young daughter or son—and survived it.

Some people might require less "heavy" reading, preferring periodically to escape their pain by reading novels, short stories, science fiction, mysteries, and the like. This kind of reading allows them to feel intense and complex emotions in an indirect, vicarious manner.

***Private Rituals.*** In addition to public rituals—like memorial services, wakes, funerals, and sitting *shiva*—that involve the community or several friends and family, there are private rituals one can perform to integrate death into life.

One common ritual is visiting the cemetery. This is a particularly helpful ritual for people who linger in the denial stage of the healing process. The denial of death can be accompanied by frequent and obsessive visits to the cemetery or by an avoidance of the cemetery altogether. In these cases, it is helpful for the grieving person to go to the cemetery "one last time." I do not intend this expression to be taken in its literal sense. Instead, I am referring to a ritual moment in which a bereaved person visits the cemetery alone to say his or her last good-byes.

Such scenes are frequently seen on TV, which often mirrors life. The person may visit the gravesite again, perhaps each year on the anniversary of the death or at some other opportune time, but this "one last time" is special because the mourner can finally get out his or her feelings and let go of the pain.

Another ritual people can use to help them deal with mourning issues is cleaning out the dead person's closet or sorting through objects the deceased family member left behind. Not everyone will be able to engage in this ritual soon after the loved one's death. Most people will need to let some time intervene before doing this task.

Sometimes, the grieving person will give some objects to family members or friends as a remembrance. Clothing and objects may be donated to a charity organization. In any case, it is helpful to dispose of the objects in a ritually loving way— one that allows the grieving person to express emotions and savor memories before "letting go" of them.

# Getting On with Life

If you truly want your children to enjoy life and the pleasures of living, you will first have to show them that life is worth living. This is not easy to do after someone dear to you has died.

To get back on track with the living, you may have to indulge yourself. For many people, this is difficult. Going out with friends to dinner or to a concert, taking in a basketball or football game, buying a new outfit, or going to the movies or a play with friends are some of the ways you might entertain yourself. At first you might feel guilty, but gradually, life itself will pull you back into the mainstream of living.

The children for whose benefit you are reading this book are an abundant source of joy. As much as you think you are reading this book for them, because you want to be a good parent or loving adult friend, I believe you also are seeking healing for yourself.

Perhaps God is gently leading you to being healed as a sign of the Creator's overwhelming love for you. As the Divine Parent, God wants you to enjoy life. And through you, God wants your children and loved ones to enjoy the world around them. In this way, you and they will be ready for the Kingdom—which is the eternal presence of joy in this world and the next!

# 7  Some Model Conversations with Children About Death

For most youngsters, the first exposure to the harsh reality of death occurs when a grandparent or other close adult relative dies. It is only natural that children demand an explanation when a loving adult who came to visit them or who lived with them is no longer around.

But often, it is during times like these that parents may find it difficult to respond to children's questions. Parents are often in grief themselves, struggling with their own sense of loss and abandonment. While seeking to protect their children from trauma, some parents may rein in their emotions. But in doing so, they cut off a healthy sharing and discussion of normal feelings. Perhaps some parents are afraid they might not say the right thing. They end up avoiding the topic altogether, leaving their child confused.

Children need to have their feelings listened to by the significant people in their lives. Then they are able to deal with feelings in a healthy manner. Children who come from the kind of family where feelings are repressed learn to imitate their parents and begin to establish a behavioral pattern that often extends to other experiences in life. Such children may become stoical in their approach to life.

Modern psychology has shown that repressed emotions have a way of resurfacing later in life. Therefore, for both the parents' and child's benefit, it is wise to deal with feelings as they arise. Open, confident, and frank discussions with the child can provide a healing and growing experience for all members of the family.

Be aware that there really are no answers or explanations that are "right" or "wrong" in all circumstances involving death. And be willing to say to a child "I don't know" when you really do not have an answer. Most children will appreciate your honesty. I have found it helpful, though, to know what other people have said and done in similar circumstances. The most effective learning occurs when people engage in a new task or when they observe a task being done by another person.

You will find support in these model conversations between children and adults about death and life after death. These conversations are based on experience and actual situations, but they have been altered to apply to a more general audience.

As you read through them, it is important to remember that these conversations must be adapted to the age level and understanding of your child.

The model conversations cover a wide variety of different circumstances: explaining the death of an adult relative to a child; explaining the death of a brother or sister; and talking with a child who is about to die.

These conversations are *not* intended to be recipes to be followed mechanically, but rather examples of what other people have done when confronted with the need to explain death and life after death to a child. They are meant to provide food for thought. Constantly be aware of your child's interest and attention level. If your child gives you any signal, verbal or nonverbal, that his or her interest or attention is waning, wind down your discussion and continue it at another time. Your own conversations will be unique and will be tailored to the special needs of your child and reflective of your own personal view of death.

## Talking about the Death of an Adult Relative

The following two conversations offer ways of explaining the illness and the death of an older relative to a child.

***Before a Death.*** Watching a member of the family slowly die is a painful experience. It puts stress on the entire family and brings up questions that are difficult to answer. Why is this happening? How can God allow another person to suffer so much? Will the loved one die?

In this conversation, note how the father maintains a hopeful, yet honest, realistic attitude toward a life-threatening illness in the family. He does not deny the possibility that the relative—Uncle Dan—might die, but he offers hope and some concrete suggestions to his child. You will also see the father's response to his child's unspoken need for physical affection and reassurance:

**Son:** Daddy, I heard Aunt Molly crying and telling Mommy that Uncle Dan is going to die! Is he really going to die?

**Father:** I don't know, Son. He's very sick and we all keep hoping and praying that he'll get better, but the way things are going, he might not. Right now, I can't tell you whether or not he will die.

**Son:** But Daddy, I don't want him to die! I love him! Why does he have to die?

**Father:** *(Hugging the child)* Well, sometimes, Son, people just get sick or hurt and die. But God takes care of them even then, because God loves them. Just like I love you and always take care of you.

**Son:** Why does God let people get sick and die? It's terrible. I love Uncle Dan and I don't want him to die. *(The child begins to cry.)*

**Father:** *(Embracing the child)* I know. I don't want him to die either, and it hurts me too to see him suffering. God doesn't make people get sick or hurt. It's just the way life is sometimes. In a way, God cries too, when someone is in pain. God tries to comfort us through other people. When we realize that people do die, it makes us a little more careful about how we treat them when they are alive. Life is very precious, so we just have to let Uncle Dan know we care about him while he is still with us, for however long that may be.

**Son:** But it makes me so sad to see him hurting.

**Father:** The doctors are doing everything they can to help him right now. Our praying for him, loving him, and comforting Aunt Molly help him, too. If he does die, we know that his suffering will be over. He'll be all right and God will care for him. Even though we will miss him, we'll know that he is not suffering anymore. But we do not know for sure that he will die, so in the meantime, we can show our love by being hopeful and by being especially kind to Aunt Molly and Uncle Dan.

*After a Death.* Often, following a death, some children seem to go on with life as if nothing at all had happened. This does not signify that the child is heartless or unaware that a relative has died. Some children just have difficulty in putting their feelings into words. Others are afraid to say anything about the death because they do not want to upset Mommy or Daddy. Children are often as protective of their parents as their parents are of them.

In the following conversation, the mother recognizes that her daughter is having difficulty talking about her grandmother's death. The mother helps the child express her feelings by first sharing her own feelings.

While you are reading this conversation, notice how this parent's openness about her feelings helps free the child to talk about her feelings. Then see how the mother tries to put the experience of death in perspective. Finally, observe how the mother backs up her attitude toward life and death with a concrete activity:

**Mother:** Sally, you know I really miss Grandma. I loved her. She was a big help to me with a lot of things. And you know, sometimes, when I just needed someone to talk to about things, she was always there to listen. You miss her too, don't you?

**Sally:** Yes, it was nice when she'd let me help her make cookies! Mommy, why did she die? You're not going to die, are you?

**Mother:** Remember how we've told you that God loves us and that someone who dies goes to heaven? Well, that's where Grandma is now! We remember her and how she loved us, and when we need to feel stronger, we can remember she would want us to be happy.

**Sally:** But Mommy, you're not going to die, are you?

**Mother:** Not for a long time—if I can help it. And by that time, darling, you'll probably be all grown up and able to take care of yourself.

**Sally:** But I'd miss you, Mommy, like I miss Grandma now. I don't want you to die!

**Mother:** I know, Sally. For you, it will be like I miss Grandma now. But you see, I knew she would die someday because everyone at some time leaves here and goes to heaven. So, you sort of prepare yourself by trying to understand and appreciate life more and more as you go along. And I have to admit that even though I'm all grown up now, I still feel very sad that Grandma is no longer here with me, but then I think about how lucky I am to have you. (Pause.) I just got a good idea. Let's go make some cookies like Grandma used to. You are a big helper now because Grandma taught you how to do it.

## Talking about the Death of a Sibling

The terminal illness of a brother or a sister is even more difficult to explain to a child than the death of grandparents or other members of the extended family. Most children can accept the fact that everyone dies eventually, but when someone so young and so close to them actually dies, the ultimate unfairness of death is acutely felt.

When a child dies, even very religious parents wonder how a loving God could allow such a thing to happen to their child. In fact, it is believed that the death of a child is the most stressful event a parent can possibly endure.

A parent who has experienced the death of a child still wants to help the surviving children. The following three conversations are based on actual interviews. What is particularly noteworthy in these conversations is the way in which each of the parents is able to be honest and realistic about what is happening, uses words a child can understand, and maintains a positive outlook.

*When a Child Is Gravely Ill.* This conversation took place before it was recognized that the child—Patty—was suffering from a terminal illness. The mother was aware that Patty was very sick, but she still was hopeful that her child would get well.

Most children, especially those between the ages of seven and twelve, want to feel useful. When they are given concrete suggestions from their parents, they develop a sense of resourcefulness and feel more in control of their own lives. Notice how the mother in this conversation encourages her son Rick:

**Rick:** Isn't God going to keep Patty from getting sick again? If the doctors can't help her get better, then God takes over, right, Mom?

**Mother:** That's right, Rick. We trust God will help Patty as much as possible, and we can pray that she will soon feel fine. In the meantime, we must do whatever we can to help Patty get well, because we love her so much. I know you'll do your best to help her by telling her you love her. Maybe you can sit with her and hold her hand sometime.

***When a Child Returns to the Hospital.*** When a child has to go into the hospital on a frequent basis, brothers and sisters might become very alarmed and begin to ask questions. Setbacks are bound to happen when a child has a life-threatening disease. In this conversation, the mother explains to Rick why surgery is not enough to help his sister Patty:

**Rick:** Why does Patty have to keep going into the hospital? I thought what the doctors did was supposed to make her all better.

**Mother:** Well, Rick, the doctors need to give her medicine to help make sure she doesn't get sick again. The doctors did everything they could to help her. But there are some things doctors cannot control. They want to take steps to stop anything bad from happening again.

*After a Child's Death.* When a child dies, it is best to tell the other children in the family about it when they are in familiar surroundings. If there are two parents in the family, both should be present to give a sense of security to the rest of the children.

Before this conversation took place, the mother and father first took their son Rick into the bedroom and sat with him on his bed before telling him about the death of his sister:

**Mother:**     Rick, Patty died today. She has gone to heaven. *(The child begins to cry and his parents hug him.)* I know you are going to miss her terribly. Your Dad and I will, too. But we're thankful that she's not hurting anymore. She's okay, now. God's taking care of her in heaven. Although she is no longer here with us, she still knows we love her.

**Rick:**     But how will she know that, Mom? And how do we know there's a heaven? And how do we know Patty's there if we can't see her anymore?

**Mother:**     Rick, we believe God loves us even though we can't see God, don't we? God shows us signs of this love every day. God gives us food to eat, people to love us, and people for us to love. God gave you and Patty to Dad and me so that we could love you. Well, if God loves us enough to show us how good it feels to love someone, God surely doesn't stop loving us after we die. And we all loved Patty— when she was sick and when she was well. She knew how much we loved her.

**Rick:**     But how will Patty know we still love her? And how do we know she's with God?

**Father:**     When you look up in the sky at night and see a shooting star or a star twinkling, you can imagine that it is Patty winking at you. If you want to show her how much you still love her, we can take flowers to the cemetery. The cemetery is the place where her body is while her spirit is with God, so it's a special place to visit her. And day after tomorrow we'll get to see her one more time at the funeral home. That's where all the people who love us and who loved her will come to say good-bye to her.

**Rick:** But how could God let Patty die? She was just three years old. She didn't get a chance to live. How could God let that happen?

**Father:** There are some things that happen that even God can't stop. This world is not perfect. Accidents happen, and people get sick and die. God doesn't make bad things happen or even let them happen. It's just the way the world is, sometimes. *(The father hugs his son closer as he speaks.)* God gives us life and the strength to live, even when it's hard to do so. That's part of growing up. We need to go on, even when things seem unfair. We'll miss Patty terribly, and we think it's terrible that she didn't get to grow up. But we also didn't like to see her in pain, and we're glad she is not suffering anymore. As hard as it was to have her die, I'm glad God gave us the chance to love her rather than not to have had her at all. And that sort of explains why this world can be the way it is. It's not perfect, but it gives us the chance to love, to grow, to learn, and to prepare ourselves to live in heaven with God forever.

# Talking about Death to a Dying Child

"Mom, am I going to die?" When a child is suffering and in pain, this is possibly the most wrenching question a loving parent can hear, particularly when the answer might be yes.

There are two conflicting schools of thought regarding whether or not someone should be told he or she is dying. One theory suggests that honesty is always the best policy and that someone should be told his or her illness is terminal.

The opposing point of view cautions that in many situations people who are told they are going to die give up hope and the will to live. Their condition rapidly deteriorates. Since miraculous recoveries do occur, telling someone that she or he is about to die may lessen the possibility for recovery.

This ambiguity about telling or not telling is compounded when a child is the focus of attention. First of all, many parents will have difficulty accepting the reality of a child's terminal illness and therefore will have a difficult time telling their child. In fact, sometimes a child intuitively knows something is wrong, long before the parents do. It may be the child who is trying to protect his or her parents from the painful truth.

Second, some children (as well as some adults) do not want to know the truth. Caring people should not force what they believe to be the truth on people who prefer to hope for the best.

Whatever the situation may be, and however you decide to approach it, it is important that you speak lovingly with the ill child, in terms she or he will understand. If the child seems to need to talk about death, don't avoid the subject.

In my experience as a minister, I have discovered that parents who regularly talk with their children about all aspects of life—including death—know best what to tell their children in such trying circumstances.

Doctors, well-meaning relatives, and friends will usually offer all sorts of opinions—often conflicting ones. Some may even offer to break the bad news for you. Even though you will want to listen to the advice of others, it is still important for you, the parents, to make the final decision.

Whatever you decide, remember that children will hear more than the words you speak. They will also hear the tone of your voice and the emotions behind your words. If you are the type of parent who has developed a comfortable and open way of communicating with your children, you will be the best expert on what your child can understand and accept.

One mother who spent three months—day and night—living in the hospital with her ill daughter, told me:

> When I saw her after she was dead, so little in the coffin, then it really hit me that she was only eleven. We talked so much while she was lying there in isolation, unable to have other visitors. She was very gifted and understood things some adults never do. So I didn't have to retell her a lot of the basics of life. She knew them already, because we always talked every day about whatever was on her mind.

Such openness and availability make a parent aware of the child's feelings and will help the parent choose whether to tell—or not to tell—the child about the gravity of his or her condition. The following conversations show how some parents made that choice.

*Not Telling the Child.* The same mother who spoke so lovingly of her relationship with the eleven-year-old child who died was asked by the child's doctors to tell the girl that she had leukemia. The mother disagreed and responded to the doctors:

> *I'm not going to tell her she's dying, and you're not, either. She has only a few months to live, and she'll be suffering enough with the treatments. She doesn't need another downer, thinking about death. No! What she needs to hear from us is about living— about the natural things of life. Death is only part of life. I'll be with her every day, every hour, while she's here in the hospital. If she has questions, I'll answer them as I always do. But we're not going to tell her something she doesn't need to hear.*

A few weeks later, the following conversation took place between this mother and her daughter.

**Child:** Am I going to die, Mom?

**Mother:** I can't tell you the answer to that question, Honey, because I really don't know for sure. I'm hopeful that you will get better. I do know if you weren't getting treatment to try to put the leukemia in remission, you would die.

You may have noted that the mother told her daughter the truth, because remissions do occur with degenerative diseases. At the same time, she admitted how serious her daughter's disease was.

> *If my daughter had had an illness that lasted longer, I would have told her, but she had only a few months to live from the time the doctors discovered the leukemia. It's not as if she had needed time to learn to live with and accept the disease.*

> *If she were older and had money of her own or a boyfriend or other relationships that she would have*

*had to deal with, it would have been different. But she was just a child, and telling her she was going to die wouldn't have made her any better. In the short time she had, she deserved to be thinking as much as possible about living, about enjoying life—not about dying!*

*While she was in the hospital, I remember the first early snow that fell. I opened the hospital window and got her some snow. She was thrilled just to be able to touch some of what was happening outside!*

***When the Child Knows.*** Many children, especially ones with long-term and life-threatening diseases, know they are dying. Often, such children accept the fact of death a lot easier than their parents do.

This can be difficult for parents, relatives, or friends to accept. The following conversation took place between a teenager who had cystic fibrosis and his parent:

**Parent:** Now, Joe, you know you must be careful. You have a serious illness and cannot expect to do what other people are doing. You just have to accept the fact and live with the limitations.

**Joe:** How dare you treat me any different from other people? I'm tired of hearing about my limitations. You're going to die someday, too. I know I'm going to die. I don't want to spend time worrying about death. I want to get on with living!

At some point, the child may need and want the parents to face reality. In the following conversation, a child tries to explain to her parents the facts of death:

**Mother:** Sandy, Dad and I bought a new rocker for your bedroom—the one you saw a few months ago and begged us to buy for you. Soon, you will be able to come home and sit in it.

**Sandy:**    Mom, you know I really am not getting any better.

**Father:**    Don't talk like that, Sandy.

**Mother:**    In no time at all, you will be home playing with your toys and entertaining your friends.

**Sandy:**    Mom, Dad. I'm really tired and my whole body hurts. I know I'm going to die. I don't want you to worry, though. The doctors keep sticking me with needles and I'm sick of it. When I die, the pain will stop. I just don't want you to be sad. I love you. *(Parents embrace their child.)*

Younger children who aren't yet capable of verbalizing their feelings may express the same kind of sentiments in their artwork. Drawings become a kind of visual conversation children have with themselves and with the significant people in their lives.

***When the Child Does Not Know.*** As discussed earlier, the agonizing decision of whether or not to tell a child that she or he is about to die is best left to the parents. Factors that might influence a parent's decision include the maturity of the child, the anticipated length of the illness, the nature of the pain or suffering to be endured, the closeness of family relationships, or the openness of communication in the family system.

Obviously, it is difficult to present one conversation that could serve as an example to cover a multitude of circumstances. The following discussion suggests one possible approach.

Notice how the parents speak with the child. The words used are directed to a child who is fairly verbal and emotionally mature. The conversation needs to be adapted to the needs and age of the child who is dying, but the general concepts are basically the same.

**Mother:** Larry, you know Dad and I love you so much, and we will always love you. We feel very lucky to have you as a son and as part of our family, because we really belong together. *(Mother hugs her son.)*

**Father:** You've been such a good, brave boy through all the treatments and pain you've had to bear with this illness. You know we've talked about how we learn something important about life from suffering and challenges. Well, I'm afraid you have to face another challenge, Son. But you are not alone in handling it. The doctors have been doing everything they can to cure you of your illness, and some of it has worked for a while. We have to be honest with you, because you've always been such a brave, honest person with us. The doctors think you're going to die from the disease.

**Larry:** I'm afraid. I don't want to die. *(Father embraces his son.)*

**Mother:** Don't worry, Son, we're going to take care of you and be with you. The doctors may be wrong. After all, doctors don't know everything yet. Many times people have surprising recoveries, and miracles do happen. Our faith tells us there is always hope. We'll keep our chins up and we'll pray.

**Father:** But you know, everyone dies at some time. You remember when Aunt Hattie died, how we talked about it? She lived a good life, and we're sure she is in heaven, enjoying being loved by God. Well, in case the doctors might be right, we thought you deserved to know, since you've always been so smart in understanding everything you've been through so far.

**Larry:** I'm going to die? I don't want to! I won't be with you anymore! I'm scared.

**Father:** I know you are scared. I am, too. But I also know that you prepare to go to heaven during this life by how you live your life. You've always been a very loving son, and together our love has gotten us through difficult times. It will get us through this, too.

**Larry:** I know Aunt Hattie went to heaven, but I don't want to go! I want to stay here with you.

**Father:** I know that, Larry. So does your mother. We want that, too. We'll be with you through this. When you were born, Mom and I felt so happy to have you. We are thankful to God for the gift you are to us. Now we have to trust that God's love for us and our love for each other will help get us through all of this. When you love somebody the way Mom and I love you, that person never dies. Love overcomes even death. Love doesn't stop. Because we love each other, we'll always be together, no matter what happens. In the same way that God has been good to you in this life, Mom and I trust God will take care of you in the next life.

**Mother:** Your dad and I want to make sure you know that no matter what happens, we'll always be with you. You remember how we explained how eternity is like a circle with God in the middle. Looking at our lives from the center of the circle, whether we're alive on earth or in heaven, it all appears to be the same time from God's perspective. So, in a way, we're already in heaven together right now. It's not like being here on earth where we have to wait. When we go to heaven, all our loved ones are already there at the same time as we are. It's all kind of mysterious to us, because it doesn't work like other things do. But in our hearts, we know it must be like that.

**Father:** It's like we said when Aunt Hattie died. Her death was only one day of her life, and we don't have to let that day overshadow all the rest of the good times we had with her. I think it's like that with everyone. Our deaths are like a temporary moment between this life and the life we live in heaven. And dying is like being reborn into an even better life.

**Mother:** So we should be doing our best in the meantime to practice what we believe—that God loves us and wants us to be happy. So we want to know what kinds of fun, exciting things you would like to do. We can still have a lot of good times together. Remember the movie *Arthur?* Arthur bought the basketball, cowboy hats, and holsters for his old butler who was very ill in the hospital so they could have some fun together. Let's do things like that! Things you would really like to do, Larry! We love you so much. For now, let's just enjoy the good things in this life and enjoy being together. Our love will get us through this together.

# Conclusion

*That is how it is with you: now you are sad, but I will
see you again, and your hearts will be filled with [joy],
the kind of [joy] that no one can take away from you.*
John 16:22

# A Fish Story with a Twist (The Author Has to Practice What He Preaches)

My son Billy won Tony at a neighborhood carnival. He had asked my wife and me if he could try to win a goldfish. With three children—ages five, four, and two—a dog, and a bird, we weren't eager for something else to take care of. Then we noticed the small openings in the fishbowls and the size of the Ping-Pong ball he would have to bounce into one of the bowls to win a fish. Thinking that it would be very difficult to accomplish, especially after watching several youngsters fail in their attempts, we told our son to go ahead and try. He got three balls for a quarter. On his very first try, a ball went into a bowl! Thankfully, his next two balls did not. But nevertheless, we now were the proud recipients of the eighth member of our family, a goldfish. Since Billy, our oldest, was only five years old at the time, we knew that much of the care of his goldfish would fall on us.

Billy was thrilled, and we were really happy for him. We cautioned him by telling him that sometimes goldfish from carnivals don't live very long, but we would take good care of the goldfish and see what happened.

Billy named the goldfish Tony. When we asked him how he chose the name, he informed us that since he didn't have any brothers, the fish must be a boy, and he liked the name Tony.

My wife Renee was pregnant with our fourth child. One of the primary reasons we had decided to go ahead and have a fourth child was to try to balance out our family, so that Billy could have a brother. This possibility made Billy very happy. Annalisa, his four-year-old sister, expressed her desire for the baby to be a girl, so that she could help take care of her. Two-year-old Chrissy said she wanted it to be a boy. Even though we stressed that we should be happy no matter what the baby was, it appeared that they each felt they would get what they wanted!

Early on the morning of October 22, 1985, my wife went into labor, and I called my wife's parents to come take care of the children. That afternoon, my wife gave birth to our third daughter, Melissa. I stayed with Renee throughout the delivery and spent some time hugging my new daughter. Then I decided to go home and meet Billy when he got off the school bus to tell him the news.

When Billy jumped off the bus, he knew I had news for him. I leaned down and put my hands on his shoulders, looked him in the eyes, smiled, and said, "Mommy had the baby today! You have a brand new baby sister."

It is amazing how quickly a child's mind can absorb a bit of information. Billy looked down at the ground and blurted out, "At least you and my fish, Tony, are boys." I digested that rather creative comment, absorbed his downcast look, and gave the old cliche a shot. "You'll really think she's cute when you see her. Aren't you happy?"

Billy grunted "yeah" as he began to run away, tears welling up in his eyes. I reached out and pulled him to me, hugged him close, and tried to reassure him. "I love you, Billy. You know we are the best of buddies. We'll just be even closer now and have lots of special times together. I really love you, my only son. I know you're going to love your new sister, too, when you see her. She really is cute. Do you want me to take you to see her at the hospital tonight?"

My son smiled briefly, fighting back his tears, and ran into the house. I followed him as he dashed into the family room and turned on the television to his favorite after-school cartoon show. He lay down on the carpet in front of the TV. I didn't bother him for a while, because I knew he needed to think.

Billy is a very intelligent, sensitive, caring youngster. Even though he was just beginning kindergarten, he could already read most of his children's books and understood things far beyond his age. He had always been very caring and loving to his two sisters and I was sure he would be fine. He just needed some time to think.

I set about the business of telephoning our friends with the good news. At least half the fun of having a new baby is telling others about it! After talking on the phone for a while, I was ready for a little break. So I got up and walked over to Tony's fishbowl.

On the very day Billy's third sister was born, the family was in for a shock! I gasped and yelled, "Billy, come here! Quick!" The fish was floating on the water.

Billy jumped up and ran over, looked, and asked, "Why is Tony swimming like that?"

I responded in a truly courageous fashion. "I don't think he's swimming, Billy! He may be dead. Fish don't swim on their sides on top of the water."

Billy, close to tears again, cried, "No! No! He's okay! See! He's moving a little!" It was true. It looked as if one of his flippers was moving slightly. I suggested that we change the water. Billy and I cautiously, carefully, and prayerfully changed the water, keeping Tony moist the whole time we were working. It seemed that Tony continued to move one flipper slightly when in the new water. I don't really think it was our imagination. But Tony didn't move any faster or more strongly, and eventually all movement stopped.

All my honest talking with Billy about the facts of death and life eternal came back to haunt me! Billy said, "Well, Tony will probably come back to life. We just have to leave him in the bowl a few days."

Hesitant to discourage Billy any further on what was not turning out to be one of his best days, I said gamely, "I don't think that will happen. It doesn't work that way. But we'll let him stay in the water for a while and see what happens. Maybe if he gets more oxygen from the new water . . . " My voice trailed off.

Fortunately, it was dinnertime. Billy was somewhat subdued during the meal. We talked about going to the hospital to see Mommy and the new baby.

Since this was the baby's first evening following birth, technically, the children were not allowed to see their new sister. But we also knew the maternity ward was on the first floor. When the mothers had the babies with them in their rooms, they could hold them by the window for the other children to see.

When Renee held Melissa by the window, thankfully, Melissa seemed to look at Billy. This won him over to her. He was immediately thrilled, thought she was adorable, and has been very happy with her ever since. He did tell me, though, to make sure Mom knew about Tony, and to ask her to pray for the fish.

The prayers did not work as we hoped, and Tony did not come back to life. Two days later, we removed Tony from the bowl. Billy put him on a paper towel and carefully wrapped him up. Having recently seen the *Bill Cosby Show* episode on TV when the whole family had dressed up for a funeral for a dead fish and then flushed it down the toilet, Billy decided he didn't like the idea of flushing Tony down the toilet. We would have to bury him instead.

We took Tony carefully out to the woods behind our house. Billy dug a shallow hole and placed Tony in it, covering him with dirt. I said a little prayer, pointing out that Tony was okay now. Billy got a couple of sticks, putting them together and placing them on top of Tony's grave. I asked, "What are you doing?"

Billy told me, "I am making a cross. That's what you have by a grave!" Then Billy decided that it was time to watch his cartoons, and the funeral was over.

When I told some of my friends this story, they asked why I did not go right out and buy Billy another fish. I had thought about doing just that. I finally concluded that if I did that, I would be teaching Billy that living things can be replaced—just like broken toys.

One of the benefits of having pets, who have shorter life spans than most humans, is that they give children the opportunity to learn about life and death, on a small scale, so that when a grandparent or some other loved one dies, they can better understand what is happening. When children care for a pet, they learn to give of themselves in a loving relationship. They learn by experience that caring requires sacrifice and responsibility, and sometimes even the pain of grief. When children experience loss at an early age, they learn that life is very precious. This is a blessing. These children will probably grow up to be wise individuals who realize that loved ones will die. This knowledge will motivate them to appreciate and love the people who are now with them.

Although the timing of Tony's death was not the best for Billy, we did not want to pretend it did not occur by quickly replacing Tony with another fish. Perhaps unknowingly, Billy had taken the risk of loving and losing a living being. In the process, he deepened his ability to care, to experience life in all of its dimensions, and finally, to deal with the loss of a loved one and still go on with life. Billy seems to have recovered from this death pretty well.

Other parents might have dealt with this situation in a completely different manner. The ultimate test of how effectively parents guide their children toward maturity, however, lies in how well their children accept death as a part of life itself. As a counselor to parents in a faith community, and as an advisor to our community's Parenting Group, I have learned it is always reassuring to point out that no one is an expert at parenting. Everyone is an amateur, learning along the way. Parents may not always say the right thing or do the right thing, but in the long run, what really counts is how well they love their children. Death makes everything seem extraordinarily important. But it is vital never to allow the times of grief to outweigh all the other experiences of life.

Billy has decided that Tony is probably swimming happily in heaven since I told him that I thought the criteria for going to heaven is to have been loved by someone else. Billy was able to grasp this concept because he had read the *Velveteen Rabbit*—a delightful story about a rabbit who became real because it was loved by a child.

In our family, new life and death arrived on the same day, reminding us that death is really the beginning of a new life. Every time someone who has loved or been loved dies, something new comes to life. That is the mystery of death and resurrection. The transition to this new life is like going from being a caterpillar crawling on the ground, earthbound, to becoming a butterfly who is free to soar up into the heavens.

# Epilogue

Gratitude must be expressed to the people whose stories and personal conversations provide authenticity for this book. Not only have they inspired me and those around them by the example of their enduring spirit in the face of the death of their children, but now, perhaps, their hard-earned insights can help many others.

I also want to express gratitude to Rabbi Harold Kushner for his landmark book, *When Bad Things Happen to Good People*. The profound and very personal insights he shared on learning how to live through the misfortunes of life and the great demand for books like his convinced me to persevere in writing this book. There is an apparent need for such works in this modern society that denies death.

I also have to thank my mother, who taught me in my childhood about God's love, and my four children, Billy, Annie, Chrissy, and Melissa, for constantly reminding me, by their questions, that parents need to have good, honest answers for their children about life and how love overcomes death. And I thank Renee, my wife, who always has the best answers, and whose love and belief in me keeps me going.

I hope your reading of this book has helped you to have the strength to look at death from the perspective of heaven, to realize that death can be overcome by the power of love, and to believe in life eternal. I further pray that you will share this faith with the children you love, because children are truly a gift to us from a loving God. In their innocence and enthusiasm, young children have not yet learned to be as earthbound as adults. They are signs to us of the joy of heaven. They deserve to know of the beautiful existence that awaits them— of which butterflies remind us.